The Long Goodbye Twice

By

Ralph Green

The two greatest loves of my life.
Rummy on my right, Delfina on
my left. Forever grateful for their
love and for the lessons they taught me.

Dedication

To all the people who helped make me who I am today.

My Mother and Father.

All my school teachers, Athletic coaches, and school staffs, who helped me get through school.

My shipmates, my fellow Firefighters, whose dedication to duty and fearless courage were and still are an inspiration to me.

And especially to Rummy and Delfina, whose unconditional love and devotion helped strengthen me spiritually and taught me what love should really be about, and whose strength and courage during the worst times of their lives, gave me the true definition of what strength, courage, and love, really are.

Acknowledgment

I would like to offer my deepest gratitude to the medical community—especially, the air crew that flew us, the staff at National Jewish Health Center, and St. Joseph's Hospital in Denver.

Their skill, compassion, and determination gave Delfina and me, **three extra, beautiful years together**.

Years filled with music, laughter, coffee in the mornings, and quiet sunsets.

There are no words that can fully express what those years meant to us, but I will always carry their gift with a grateful heart.

I cannot thank them enough.

Contents

Chapter 1
Where to Begin?

That's always the question, isn't it?

Rootin', Tootin', Shootin', Ralph

Here seems a good place.

As an eight-year-old boy, in Roswell, New Mexico, you just don't realize that God is already preparing you for something much bigger than yourself.

But in reflecting back over my life, that is when it started.

When I was a happy go-lucky eight-year-old, not realizing the struggles of my parents, I had no clue what was happening. I never felt poor, but we were. We had a place to live, though we moved around a lot inside the city of Roswell. It never dawned on me why. Sometimes, we'd move into a smaller house and a worse neighborhood, but to me they were all the same. I met other kids, as poor as me and we made friends, played together, wore the same ragged clothes. None of us knew the difference. And that made us richer than we'd ever be again.

My father, God rest his soul, was a chronic alcoholic, who could support his habit, but not his family. He could always find a way to get enough to buy his vice.

My Dad used to go as far as to talk me out of my lunch money to buy his vice. La Capita. A local cheap wine that sold for fifty-five cents a pint, back in the late fifties and early sixties.

When he did work, it was farm labor, cotton gins. Things that a migrant worker would do also. He would work just long enough to buy a day or two's worth of his La Capita, then lay-up drunk or hang out with his drinking buddies, who only came around when he had something to drink. I heard words that I got soap in the mouth for repeating, when his buddies were around, so I learned to keep a distance from them, so I couldn't hear those things. Mom never had to ask where I heard them. She just made sure I didn't use them in public.

Before the Nursing home days, we had an old Hudson. I used to go riding with him, not knowing his condition could affect his driving. He would use me to con money off his friends, saying he needed fifty-five cents for my lunch money the next day, or a meal that night. Yes, you could get a meal for fifty cents back then.

Three different times, he stopped to get a gallon of gas to get home on, at different gas stations. I'd run to the bathroom, and he'd just drive off and leave me there. He didn't miss me until Mom asked where I was. Then the search was on. The gas station attendants would realize what happened, but there were no cell phones back then. I didn't know my home phone at that time, or if we even had one. Sometimes we did, sometimes we didn't. It just depended on which bills got paid that month. A phone in the house, back then, was a luxury, not a real need. If mom couldn't yell loud enough to get me home, then she'd go looking. I learned to stay within earshot to keep my butt from hurting when she found me.

So, the attendants were great. They would let me play around the station, hoping someone would come looking for me. Sure enough, eventually, the sound of the old Hudson could be heard from a few blocks away, and it would come rolling up to the pumps again, mom at the wheel, retracing the possible route my dad may have taken. They pulled up to the pumps and would spot me, I made sure of that. My mother would be crying, happy to find me, while at the same time, cursing out my dad for leaving me, and her having to come up with a dollar for gas to make the trip.

One night, she told Dad he could not take me with him, since his track record was terrible when it came to child care.

Dad came walking home later that night and without a word, went into the bedroom and passed out into a drunken sleep. Nothing out of the ordinary. He'd often get so drunk, even he knew he shouldn't drive and walk home. We'd spend most of the next day looking for the old Hudson. This night would be a bit different.

At around three the next morning, three law enforcement officers knocked on our door.

Mom answered in her robe and pillow hair.

"Pardon us, ma'am, do you own a green Hudson?"

"Why yes, why?"

"Who was driving it last?"

She answered, "My husband."

They asked where he was.

She told them he's here.

With a look of surprise, the lead officer said: "Is he alive?"

As it turned out, Dad had been driving the back roads, drunk, of course, and had miss negotiated a turn, rolled the old Hudson an estimated five times, then got out and calmly walked home. If he'd been sober, it probably would have killed him.

He got to spend the night in jail, and Mom went and bailed him out the next morning, which she would do on a regular basis throughout their marriage. He did ask as she bailed him out; "Was Ralph with me? I don't remember bringing him home." I have many tales of what happened while dad was drinking, but that's best left for another memoir.

So, the duty of supporting the family got passed off to my mother, who took it up with an entrepreneurial gusto and started her own business. She was a nurse, who worked part time at doctors' offices and waited tables, to make ends meet.

No baby sitting back then either. I'd go and sit quietly in the lobby, or in case of the Diners she worked at, I'd be retired to a back corner booth, with a hamburger, French fries, and a Coke until her shift was done. I'd always bring my comic books, which I actually learned to read from, before I started school. They helped develop a comical wit about me, which some of my teachers would later come not to appreciate. My mom was doing the best she could with what she had to deal with. She always stood as a shield between the real world and me and my sister, so we wouldn't be exposed to any more of the ugliness of alcoholism than need be.

She wanted something better, so when I was eight years old and in school, she started a nursing home.

This became Gods original training ground for me to prepare me for my most important task in life.

I should note an important detail. It was originally located two blocks away from Roswell's central fire station, where my cousin's husband worked. This had a significant effect on my future, as it planted a seed of wanting in my heart.

My mother couldn't afford to hire help, so I learned a lot about caregiving as an eight-year-old boy.

I found the old people delightful. I would listen to their life stories and advice, as I made their beds, fed them and tended to their other needs, as best an eight-year-old could do, which most said I did fine.

I got quite an education and I knew things the other kids at school had no idea about. World War I and World War II. The Bataan Death March. The reason a Ford was a terrible vehicle and Chevrolet was "America's Car."

I learned about Arthritis, emphysema, and a host of other ailments. My teachers knew nothing of the education they were giving me. They were just talking about the wonderful lives they had lived, and some of the not so wonderful parts of them.

Some had to adjust to the idea of a child helping change their diapers and clothing, but we all got used to it, and life went on.

This was also my first introduction to Alzheimer's disease, which at that time was known only as senility and an expected condition of old age. Of course, at eight, everyone was "old" to me. Though looking back, some of them were very young to have developed it. In their sixties and seventies.

I just couldn't understand how anyone, at any age, could just forget their entire life. Their children, grandchildren, spouse. Everything.

I prayed a lot throughout the years, that it would never happen to me.

What did I know? I knew that life wasn't fair.

I met old war heroes, who, when I first met them, had tales to tell of where they'd been, what they'd done.

Some even shared how they won the medals they had displayed on their night stands. Then a year later, these same heroes, didn't remember even going to war, or being in the service. They would give me a blank stare, when I asked them to tell me that story again of a battle they'd shared, only months before, and the silence that followed.

It was heartbreaking to experience, but it did give me a value of life and what was important, even at that young age. So, hang on to your memories, because they might not hang on to you.

Every time one of them would pass on, it was like losing a grandparent. They weren't just clients. My mother was old fashioned. They ate what we did and were treated with the respect their age had earned them. They were family.

With that context explained, that was my life, until I was nineteen.

Of course, I went to school, played sports, worked as much as I could on farms and other things to try to break the mold, but I kept getting drawn back to the home.

My mother expanded her business. Sometimes, she had as many as three houses, close to each other. I built some strength moving the old, heavy hospital beds from room to room, house to house. Lifting patients to change them or get them ready for the day.

I was glad I was doing the hard farm work, mostly in the evenings and night. Bailing hay isn't done in the New Mexico sunshine. It helped me build the strength needed to help Mom out at the home.

I played football, wrestled (district Champion two years in a row), threw the shot put in track. I even sang in the high school choir. Anything for some time away from "work," which I actually never saw it as work. It was all just a way of life.

I did participate in a High school Chorus play *"South Pacific,"* which made an impact on my young mind as to what a sailor's life might be like.

"We've got sunlight on the sand; we've got moonlight on the sea..." you can see the influence.

That and my American history teacher, who was a retired Navy Senior Chief, whose tales of his adventures around the world, gave me a bit of a wanderlust and a possible means to see the world.

He told of visits to places I just knew I could never see. The Bahamas, Virgin Islands, Italy, Spain. He'd been to Japan and all around the world.

Somehow, he ended up retiring in Roswell, teaching High School American History. Telling tales that made young boys want to become sailors.

I felt like I was going to be trapped in Roswell and the Nursing home forever. We were better off than before, but with the business came expenses. Mom never let on about her struggles to keep all the bills paid, but looking back, there were obvious indicators of financial strife.

I had started grade school a year behind, due to my February birthday, so I didn't graduate high school, until I was nineteen.

What happened at nineteen? Everything!

I graduated High School, got married, pregnant (at least my future wife did) and joined the Navy all within a three-month Period.

I met my future wife in High School. A pretty, Auburn haired, sweet looking young (too young) girl in a mini-skirt, with long legs, who told me I couldn't sit in the desk I had picked out. I had transferred in from another class, and the occupant was skipping class that day. I said; "Oh come on, beautiful. I'm just trying to sit as close to you as I can. Give me a break."

Well, a break she gave me. And a date. One thing led to another, and we eventually had to, and wanted to get married, above many objections from the adults in our lives. But I was taught a code of honor by my mother, and I did what a man should do. I married her and joined the Navy at nineteen. She was 17 at the time. A match built for disaster, but who knew?

The marriage lasted nine years, and ended at the end of my Navy career. I got two fantastic sons from my first wife, Allen and Troy, and a rough life lesson. My boys are worth it though.

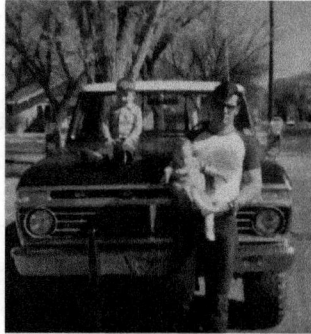

Me. Home on leave with my boys.

I did get to see them more now, than I would have dealing with constant deployments, so it was the right thing for me to do, returning to civilian life. I got to watch them grow, join the Air Force, get their educations on their own merit, I might add, I was too broke to pay for their college. They did me proud.

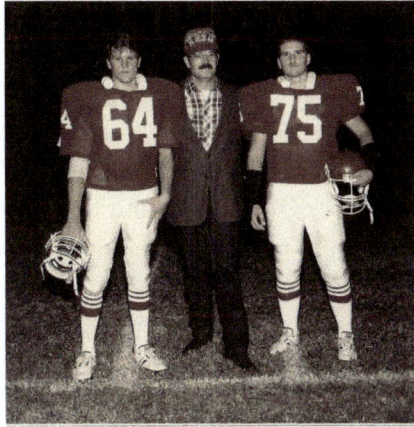

Troy, Me, and Allen on Parents' Night

I won't say anything bad about their mother. Neither of us were really ready for marriage at that age, but we were at the age that we knew everything there was to know and no one could tell us different. Man, did we get an education, that first year, especially.

Who's FICA? Why is he taking all my paycheck? Wait, you have to pay for electricity, gas, and water? Who knew? We found out. The Navy treated us well. We had food, a place to live and once again, friends that all dressed the same as me. There was no fashion competition, and we all lived in the same neighborhood. Life was good in those early years.

Here's a cute cost comparison: Allen cost seven dollars and twenty-five cents to be delivered. He was born in an Army hospital.

Troy cost an even seven dollars. It cost less to feed his mother in the Navy hospital he was born in, two years later. Her meals, for four days, was all I had to pay for the deliveries were free.

They were worth every penny. Such blessings to my life.

Chapter 2
In The Navy

The Navy truly was an adventure, but as it turned out, it too was meant to prepare me for God's plan and help give me the means to do what I had to do, later in life. It taught me patience, above all and a dedication to duty.

I made too many wonderful friends to mention them all, but I will say, I got used to working with people who were willing to lay down their lives for their shipmates, God, country and their quest for world peace. We always had each other's backs. There were no different races, cultures, or ethnic groups. We were all literally on the same boat. If she went down, she'd show no bias to race, color or creed. Whatever happened to her, happened to us all, as one group. To the ship and the rest of the world, we were just American sailors. We all knew where we stood. We stood together.

I got used to working with people who would die for you, with you, or to defend the freedom of the world we were living in. We were constantly being put in harm's way for countries that didn't even seem to like us, but we all understood the bigger picture. We were serving a greater purpose than just our own needs and wants. We were making a difference.

I did some shore duty at Compatwing 11 communications center in Jacksonville, Florida.

I came there directly from Radioman A and C school in Bainbridge, Maryland. My first son, Allen, was born there at the Army's Aberdeen Proving Grounds, since the NTC didn't have a hospital. I went to the morning inspection with Cigars wrapped in "It's a boy!!" wrappers stuffed into my Dixie cup sailor hat. Everyone laughed and congratulated me. Proud Papa.

Back to Jacksonville.

That's where I saw the first computer I'd ever seen. It was HUGE!!! It took up the largest room in the building. I couldn't believe they'd let a nineteen-year-old kid touch it, let alone start training me to operate it. We had civilian workers, who were highly skilled technicians that did the day-to-day stuff on it, but we got to troubleshoot it when it displayed error codes, input data cards, and all the other busy work type stuff.

Then the message processing center. I'd never seen a multilith printing press before either, but within a few days of my arrival, I was taking it apart for cleaning, troubleshooting paper jams, using it to print thousands of classified and other documents with it. It was totally fascinating.

I ended up spending most of my time back in "air to ground," where I did safety of flight duties for P3 Orion's, because of my Morse code skills I had improved on in "C" school. I was one of the last classes that was required to learn Morse code, so we quickly became the dinosaurs of the fleet. Even the P3's eventually migrated to teletypes.

As a Petty Officer third class, the money wasn't just rolling in, and I had a wife and two children to support, so I took a part time job at the on base horse stables, since I had a love for animals due to all the farm work I used to do. We had thirty-two horses to care for. Fourteen owned by the stables for rental and the rest were privately owned. I enjoyed being around them so much that when it came time to re-enlist, I did it on horseback. The Navy at the time, would try to accommodate you with wherever you wanted to re-enlist. So that was that. Just some interesting trivia.

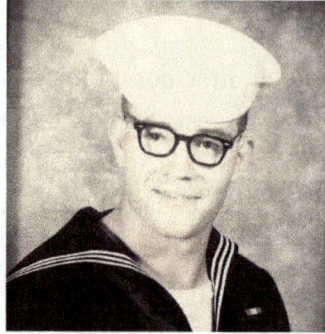

My Boot camp picture

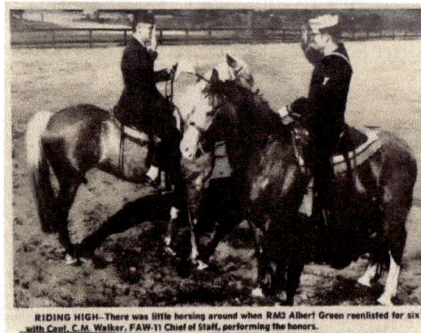

RIDING HIGH—There was little horsing around when RM3 Albert Green reenlisted for six
with Capt. C.M. Walker, FAW-11 Chief of Staff, performing the honors.

Me. Re-enlisting on horseback.

I did make two trips completely around the world and many other shorter deployments. I did get to see the Bahamas, the Virgin Islands, Italy, Spain, Japan, and the rest of the world, just as my American History teacher had described, aboard my home for almost four years, the USS Independence: CV 62.

It didn't take long being aboard her to realize why all sailors refer to their ships as "She." She quickly becomes the most beautiful and important thing in your life. She never lets you down. She's always ready for a trip. She loves adventure, and she's VERY high maintenance and expects a LOT out of you in return for keeping you afloat.

USS Independence CV 62 (The Indy)

The sleeping quarters weren't quite the equivalent of a cruise ship, but she got us where we needed to be to protect world freedom. She became my "home" for almost four years. I spent more time on her, out at sea, than I did at home. My house became my "home away from home" and the Indy became a more familiar refuge for me. I knew what I had to do and when to do it. Three hots and a cot. Everyone had the same goal. Get the job done and survive another day.

Being aboard an aircraft carrier taught me more lessons than I can list. But one thing I learned was I could sleep anywhere, anytime, day or night, no matter what.

My berthing area was nicknamed "Skid Row" due to the abundance of piping and cables running through it that made it look more like an alley than a sleeping area.

And it was located just below the forward catapult water brakes on the 03 level — the first deck below the flight deck. When a plane is launched, something has to stop the catapult. When it hits those brakes, it sounds like a freight train collision. Every two minutes.

Flight operations normally run twenty-two hours a day while at sea. We played war-games constantly, so we were always in a state of alert. There was no waiting for those quiet, peaceful moments to catch a nap. I learned you could get a two-minute catnap while standing up, leaning against a steel bulkhead, and then continue working for twelve more hours.

We were always undermanned in my division when we set sail. We always got the same promise. "We'll pick up some newbies once we get underway. The newbies never showed up. So, we slept when we could, where we could.

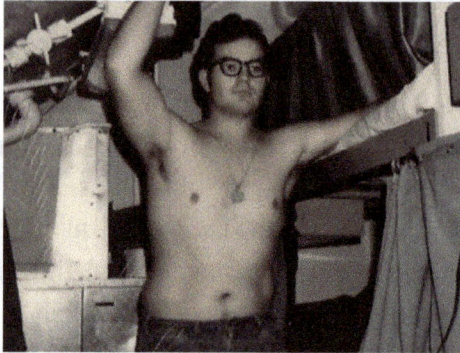

Me, by my rack in "Skid Row"

We had billets for one hundred seventy men in my division. (Communications) but we ran with forty-percent of that on all but one cruise, where we actually left Norfolk, fully manned.

We seemed to accomplish more and win more awards while undermanned than when we had a full crew. We were too busy to get in each other's way. Everywhere you looked, people were working. Busy, just trying to keep up with what was going on. Fully manned, you would see people standing around, looking for "busy" work to keep them occupied and out of the sight of the Senior Chief. If he saw the standing around, they would be put to work or volunteer to help out in the mess decks, so, just grab a swap and keep the freshly swabbed deck clean and look busy. That was the key to an easy day.

We won the Green "C" Battle Efficiency award one year with only forty-two percent manned.

I did make rank quickly, because of being in a "critical" Rate. I made Petty Officer second class (E5) in less than two years. You had to have at least eighteen months of service to qualify for the rank. I made Petty Officer First class (E6) with just over three years of service and would remain that rank, though it would change to Staff Sargeant in the National Guard, until I retired from the military service in 1994 after twenty-one years of total service.

Me on duty in FACCON

We had our motto posted in the area I worked, Facilities Control, (FACCON) for the entire time I was aboard. It's an old handed down motto, not really original, but fitting.

"We have done so much, with so little, for so long, that we can now do anything, with nothing, forever."

We did a lot of traveling. The Navy keeps that promise. You will see the world and it will see you.

Some of the views were totally outstanding. The Navy says you'll see the world and I certainly did. It's eighty percent water, but I saw it!!

I got to cross the equator and become a "Shellback." I sailed in the Arctic Ocean and became a "Blue Nose." I got to see the wonders of the Mediterainian many times. The ten day trip across the North Atlantic was always facinatingly beautiful.

Cuba, the Florida Keys, Bahamas, Virgin Islands, the Azores and may other places, I'd never even heard of. It was the tour of a liftime.

On the Flight Deck, rebuilding an antenna

On the catwalk getting fresh Mediterranean air

I was a Radioman in the Navy. I was on the internet while it was still known as the Worldwide Mobile Communication System. In later years, it became part of the internet. Computers were still huge and expensive. I'd never seen one until I joined the Navy.

The change in technology during the nine years I was in the Navy happened daily, will take another book to cover the amazing pace at which the changes took place.

But one amazing thing that did happen that deserves a note here, the first time I set sail on the Indy, we communicated with total Low to UHF frequencies and had to keep them ten percent apart due to frequency harmonics. Picture instruments being off key and ruining the music. Same thing. We communicated with the rest of the world mainly using HF, which is subject to the whims of the sun and the atmosphere. We had to learn to read those whims and adjust frequencies every hour or two to keep ahead of them. The frequencies had to be clear enough to support Frequency Shift Keying modulation to support our sixty and one hundred word per minute teletypes. We were still transitioning to the higher speed. Morse code had been shifted to monitoring emergency frequencies only

Midway into the cruise, we put into port and a crew came onboard and fitted us with satellite equipment. They said they put up a communications satellite called the "gap filler" in space for military use only. They said it would be like dragging a landline around with us, twenty-four-seven.

We even got two twelve hundred word per minute printers to keep up with it.

And it did just that. For five whole days. Then Mother Nature sent a meteorite to destroy the main antennae, and reduced it to only being accessible eight hours a day. Still, we had learned to use whatever we had available and could still operate just fine the "old fashioned" way.

We ended up the cruise with a stopover in the Virgin Islands, then back into the Portsmouth shipyards for more work and refurbs to get us ready for sea again.

When we pulled back out, we had eighteen hundred word per minute printers, five satellite antennae, and twenty-five brand new satellites in orbit, that we could access twenty-four-seven.

That still amazes me. We were only in the ship yards for three months.

One other little thing. When we left on that cruise, which lasted nine months, I had a sweet collection of eight track tapes and some nice eight track players in my pickup and house. The ships store quit carrying eight tracks three months into the cruise. These little rectangular shaped things called cassettes started showing up in their place.

I didn't give it much thought until we got back home. There was not an eight-track tape, player or system of any kind, anywhere to be found. Just gone!! It took me longer to adjust to them being gone than it did for them to just disappear. That shocked me more than the satellite communication system being developed and put in place in only three months.

My time in the Navy was like nowhere else on earth. We got to experience the wonders and beauty of nature, the advances in technology all while knowing we were making a difference.

On one Mediterranean cruise, we had two catastrophes.

One: We had an obnoxious Admiral onboard, who totally disrespected our Captain, in front of the crew, several times before leaving port.

Two: Because the Admiral actually took over command, when our Captain told him he would not sail the route the Admiral wanted to take, because of there was a hurricane already in the path on that one, and we all knew it. He sailed us right up the middle of it, because big ships can weather storms. He took the helm, our Captain restricted himself to quarters and away we went.

You're just not supposed to see waves breaking thirty feet over the deck of an Air Craft carrier, as it's already forty-eight-feet above the water line. We had a two-day break going through the eye of the storm, and then back at it.

Forty-five degrees of list is considered capsize list for that particular ship. We got hit by some HUGE waves from the port side (due to improper commands from the Admiral) and listed at forty-three degrees for over an hour and a half, before a real helmsman finally got us back upright. It's the only time I ever had to walk on the bulkhead and the deck at the same time to get across the workspace.

We made it through the storm, the captain took back over, and the Admiral was relieved of his command, when we arrived in Rota, Spain. His career was over.

Six weeks moored in Naples, Italy. We had to hire local national companies to help repair the over three million dollars in damage to the ship, due to treaties of the time. We couldn't just call in tender or the Seabees to use as labor. We used to have twenty-one thirty-five-foot deck edge antennae, bigger than a telephone pole all around the ship. We did not have one left when we got to Spain. We lost seven full antennae platforms and fifty feet of solid steel catwalks.

When the waves outweigh your ship, things happen.

Never underestimate the power of water.

This is a small part of the damage. Solid steel, bent to the extreme. The Thirty-five foot antennae that they supported are just gone to Davy Jones, never to be seen again. Scattered along

Miles of the bottom of the North Atlantic Ocean. Undiscovered icons of a trip that could have been avoided, except for an Admirals ego. It all worked out. Karma takes care of things.

Stormy Prayers

Dedicated To the USS Independence CV-62

Life has been different since that day, Out on the deep blue sea.

We look at things with new respect,

My shipmates and me.

The sea shifted from blue to black, In such a short, short time.

We could see her waves by looking up, As our lives ran through our minds.

With such deep thought about our past, Our futures came into play.

With the sea so rough we walked the walls, Even atheist would pray.

For three long days and endless nights We thought our lives had been in vain, Then came the answer to our prayers, The end of the hurricane.

Ralph Green

Copyright ©2005 **Ralph Green**

At nineteen years old, it's a dilemma. You think you know everything in the world. All adults are stupid and you try not to admit their advice is beginning to make sense. I've had many such occasions in my young life, so when I had so many adults agreeing that I was making a good choice by joining the Navy, it was a bit confusing, but I did it anyway.

I did tell my mother, a few years later; "Mom, when I was a teenager, you were probably the stupidest person I knew. You never made any sense at all. It's amazing how much more intelligent you and your words have become, the older I've gotten. Truly miraculous."

I still remember her smile and laugh at that.

I chose to join the Navy, not knowing what really lay in store, I even reenlisted once because I felt a sense of pride and honor connected to my service and truly had a deep love and devotion to this nation of ours. Especially after being able to compare it to all the nations I got to visit. It's the best!! If you ever want to really appreciate America, take a tour of almost any country in the world, even as close as Mexico. You'll get a whole new perspective.

But I did not recognize what a gift from God it was until much later in life.

The sailor's life gave me a totally different perspective of the world than I had before and I think different from how most civilians see it. We, especially as Americans, forget what a small circle of the world we live in. Even with the World Wide Web giving us stark reminders daily.

It also gave me a work ethic that last until this day. And unknowingly, the firefighting training the Navy gave me would qualify me for my dream career.

Both jobs would teach me how to listen to needless criticism, angry people, and direct insults without blowing a fuse. A lesson in tolerance needed when caring for advanced Alzheimer's victims. Even the "nicer" ones, like Rummy. She had her moments.

I missed my boys and family during deployments, typically nine months a year, so I made my decision to get out of the Navy to be closer to them.

After a very dramatic divorce, I did get visitation and got to be with them more as a civilian. The new adventures that lay ahead, showed me it was the right choice.

Chapter 3
Fire Department and Part-Time Jobs

I had a few jobs before getting the one I'd always dreamed of. As I mentioned earlier, my mom started her nursing home two blocks from the Roswell Fire Department's Central Fire station. My frequent visits there started my dream of one day becoming one of them. They would show me the fire trucks and equipment, take me for rides and even let me watch their television, which very few people had back then. Even then, I felt very lucky that they just sort of took me in.

I'll get back to the other jobs later, as one was a very important factor in meeting my future wives.

But I did apply and got chosen to be a Roswell New Mexico Firefighter, but the waiting list had fifteen people on it. I was number five, so I'd have to wait almost ten months. They made a new list every year, so, I cut it close, but was elated when the call came in. I was already getting into shape to take the hiring test again. The written was easy. The Fire Combat Challenge was exactly that. Physically challenging. I found it interesting. Doable, but interesting.

That career would span twenty years. I won't tell the thousands of war stories about the Navy or the ones from my fire service, but there were many. Each one taught me a new lesson in life and about humanity, but again, I fell in with a unique group of individuals, that no matter what our differences in the rest of the world, we would put our lives on the line for each other, have each other's backs, and put ourselves in harm's way, yes, even die to save people we didn't know and property we didn't own. We did it for the love of our community and the world in general. If you know anything about firefighters, at that time especially, a beginning firefighters pay still put them at poverty levels. So, no. Not one of us did it for the money. Once again, I was in a group that were all at the same income level and we all dressed alike. No race, color or creeds here. Fire has no bias or prejudices. It burns you all the same. The other emergency situations do the same.

Much like the Navy, we had to all keep a part time job to put beans on the table. I learned to weld at our local campus on my GI bill, and once again, worked on some of the local dairy farms in the area, fixing what the cows would break. I just couldn't stay away from farms. I loved the animals and the people too much. It takes very special people to farm in this mass production world.

I also cut trees and sold firewood. I was quite the woodsman. I cut trees from places most people wouldn't touch. I climbed to the top, chainsaw in hand, and took them apart, as you can't just drop a tree that's between three houses, a fence and a tool shed. I had to cut them in smaller, more manageable pieces and rope them to the ground.

Such a great combination of skills. My woodcutting was enhanced by the fact that I could weld. It's easier to sell split wood, than huge solid blocks. Once again, being poor is the mother of ambition. I couldn't afford to keep renting small wood splitters that just couldn't do the job of splitting the type of wood I was cutting, so I had to design, fabricate and build my own. Challenge accepted!!

Here's my wood splitter, built from my junk pile and an old 1974 Toyota Carolla and a Green Chile roaster that I built from my junk pile. There is no such thing as scrap metal, when you're poor and can weld.

Sixty-four tons of hydraulics, a five-inch cylinder with a twenty-four-inch throw. A twenty-four-inch-tall wedge, and a twenty-four-inch-tall pusher built of inch and a half steel with three-quarter-inch steel side supports, powered by a 1974 Toyota Corolla engine. Built from metal out of my spare parts pile. And a Chile roaster I built, just because Dudley bet me I couldn't. His grandson has the latter now.

New Mexico is famous for it's red and green chilies, just for some context as to why I would need or want such a contraption. We used to roast between five and seven bushels of green chilies a year, just for me and Rummy. I would roast more for the rest of the family, as needed, including what Delfina and Dudley would consume.

My One Bushel Chile Roaster.

My little log Splitter

Firefighter/EMT was a labor of love. Because I was both techy and mechanical minded and love to help others, it was the perfect match for me. Someone once said, "If you love what you're doing, you'll never work a day in your life." I have found that to be so true. I was very blessed in that respect. I've always managed to fall into jobs I loved doing. God has guided me well.

I did learn that there was more to being a Firefighter/EMT than just putting the "wet stuff on the red stuff." Firefighting is a science and being an EMT requires certification and physical ability as well. I did use a portion of my GI bill to go to our local collage and get an AA in Fire Science as well as my welding certificate. I was officially diversified. A true labor portfolio.

But so was everyone I was to work with within the department. The skillsets within the department had a wide range. Contractors, Nurses, skilled labor, eventually, even a Lawyer. If you needed anything built or whatever your task, call your local Fire Department, and see if someone there can do it. You won't be disappointed.

Once again, I was working with a group of people who would lay down their lives for people they'd never met before in their lives. People who don't understand that mentality, need not submit a job application.

They would literally die with you, before leaving you behind and alone. They would die for you, put themselves in harm's way. No checking the color of your skin, religious beliefs, political affiliation, mental health status, legal background, or financial standing, just because it's the right thing to do.

I've always said, "Our job is to save people we don't know from trouble we didn't cause, and save property we don't own."

Our jobs were also to intervene in other people's tragedies. We couldn't always make things better, but we did our best to keep them from getting any worse.

We're not special. We're not heroes. We're just people who try to do the right thing, at the right time. And that's a delicate combination.

Not "special." That's a reminder of this story. It's still on track. About a training captain who came out to visit my ARFF crew at the airport's fire station four one day.

Back then, we had several members of the crew who smoked. We had just had to rename our crew and trucks from the "Crash" crew and our trucks to "Crash" one and two, to the ARFF (Aircraft Rescue and Fire Fighting) crew and our trucks to ARFF unit one and two.

Funny, but it seems pilots didn't like to hear the phrase "Roswell tower, Crash one and two are en route. Or anything on the radio with the word "Crash" in it, so we joyfully complied.

Part of the compliance was to repaint the large ashtray frame that had large, fat letters that said, "Crash Station 4" on it, to read "ARFF STATION 4." We painted it in large fat letters again, but in a nice bright red.

That same day, the training captain, who knew very little about ARFF as it was at the time, very specialized training, came for a visit.

As we poured coffee and sat down at the table, his eyes fixed on the ashtray.

"What the hell is this? Do you guys really think you're something special? You're just firemen, like the rest of us, not special at all. If anyone is special, it's my rescue crews. They

28

make every call that comes in." (special note: I drove the "Rescue" unit for two years and never felt "special")

So, the visit was brief, to say the least. And we didn't talk about much.

Our next shift was two days later. He came back out for another visit. His eyes again immediately fixed on our newly painted ashtray again. It now read "JAFFS" and he ask, "Now, just what the hell does that mean? Are you putting yourselves into an even more special group now?"

To keep it PG, we told him, "Nope. That stands for "Just Another Frickin' Fire Station." He blushed, even. The visit went better than the last. We actually talked about ARFFF training for everyone, at least the basics, as our back-up crews needed some knowledge while we were out on any call. We responded to all emergencies in the center, structure, EMS, and any other emergency, not just the flight line. Every time he'd visit after that, he'd look at that ashtray and smile.

I went one step further. I put JAFFF (Just Another Frickin' Fire Fighter) on the back of my helmet. No one special. Just one of the crew.

My email, to this day, is jafff@jafff.com. Yes, the domain is mine.

Me. At Fire Station Four at Rosell's Airport

Me at a Training Fire

Many of the same group. It's sadly, gotten smaller over the years.

Yes, we still get togther.

We can sit like we used to in the fire station. We can talk about the things we've done, the lives we saved, the ones we couldn't, without anyone getting shocked or offended, because we lived each of the stories we tell together and survived to pass the stories on, if only to each other, as when you get home, they're just too tramatic to share with a family of "normal" people. My family told me when they'd had enough. "Please don't tell the gory details."

There are things you just keep to yourself until you get back to the station around people who understand. I called it coffee table therapy. We would sit and review what just happened, what we did right, and what we did wrong. What we could have done different. Or better. How did our arrival on the scene change it. Did we make things better after arriving on scene? It was both thereaputic and productive. Things a "normal" person wouldn't want to hear or understand.

Much like Spock told McCoy, in Star Trek IV: The Voyage Home, when he asked about his death experience; "It would be impossible to discuss the subject without a common frame of reference."

That's exactly how I feel when a "normal" person asks me to explain or talk about all the death, destruction, and mayhem I've encountered in my life. I have quoted that line more times than I can remember.

I'm sure others have developed similar comebacks to questions people really don't want to hear the answers to, but it doesn't stop them from asking. If you do try to explain, they usually stop you and say, "OK. You're right. That's enough.

It's a familiarity that we, a group of retired Firefighters, with a combined experience of over three hundred years, all share, every other month over breakfast and coffee. "Normal" people see us as just a group of old guys sitting around a table talking too much or ignore us completely. We don't mind, either way. We're a bunch of "Just Another Frickin' Fire Fighters," and we enjoy being healthy enough to do this bi-monthly therapy session.

My training as an EMT would really come in handy in the years after retirement as well. It seems we don't always know what lies ahead of us, and we so rarely pay attention to the road we've traveled that we forget we are here for a reason, and we're not just a random grouping of cells and DNA. We are here, mainly, for each other. In My Humble Opinion.

God made sure I was ready to take on what he had in store for me, later in life, and he let me love what I was doing as a bonus, and I thank him daily for that. I have met people who are miserable in their jobs, and I'm so grateful not to be one of them.

As a Firefighter/EMT, you're just not supposed to sit around and wish that you were busier. To do so is like wishing tragedy on other people, so we try not to do that. The trucks and equipment are constantly needing maintenance and upgrading. The station can always use a good cleaning. We never want the coffee pot to feel ignored. There was always training to keep our skill levels honed to a sharp perfection, as our working envirinment was never in a forgiving mood. Mistakes in the field cost more than just money. Injury, death, and mayhem are always on the menu. We always did our best to keep those at a minimum.

For a Quiet Shift

*To those I met on and off duty who made such a difference in my
life.*

As I sit in the station for what seems the millionth time,

once again, the shift ahead keeps running through my mind.

Is this time I have to offer,

ever going to be enough?

I know today I'll meet some folks who really have it rough.

Will it be a fire, or perhaps more EMS?

Will it be a MVA,

or some other bloody mess?

A small voice inside me

hopes for a quiet shift,

One, where people get along

and give my heart a lift.

My concentration's broken

as I hear the alarm tone.

Another wish for a quiet shift

is just as quickly gone.

Ralph Green

Copyright ©2005 **Ralph Green**

Chapter 4
Me and the National Guard

Having served nine years in the Navy, I knew I didn't just want to flush that time down the toilet.

The National Guard seemed like the best alternative to me, as there was no Navy Reserve unit near Roswell.

I took a few months to get things together and joined. It was an exciting time.

The unit, the First and 200th ADA, had a heroic heritage of being one of the units that made the Bataan Death march during World War 2.

I held many positions there. Military intelligence, Ground Air Observer, Division Air Management Element (DAME) NCO, Reconnaissance Selection and Occupation of Position (RSOP) NCO, Squad Leader of an M42 Duster squad, and squad leader of a Chaparral tracked air defense missile system, and many other extra-curricular duties.

Military Intelligence is said to be a conflict in terms. I found it fascinating. Determining how many and what types of troops and units are in the area by the cigarette butts and other paraphernalia they leave behind was always interesting.

In today's world, of course, we would rely heavily on satellite photos and thermal imaging to make those SWAG (Scientific Wild Ass Guesses), but back then, it was a true science.

As RSOP NCO, it was my squad's duty to make sure the new area we were moving to was safe and free of all nuclear, biological, and chemical weaponry.

That meant we always went into the area first wearing full chemical gear. (MOP 4) and took the instruments we needed to test for every chemical known to man.

Our PFC asked me one time; "Sarge, why do you always call me Canary? I mean, it's a cute nickname and all and it's not offensive, but does it have a meaning?"

I told him, "Sure. Canary isn't a nickname; it's a title. It's slang for you're our hero in real times of actual combat."

He asked, "How so?"

"Well, when we get to the new zone, haven't you noticed, I always let you take your chemical gear off first?"

He said, "Well, not until now. I just thought you were being nice to the new guy."

"Nope, that's not it at all. If you remember, coal miners always took a canary down into the mines with them. If the canary died suddenly, it was a hero, as it saved all their lives. They would turn around and go back. That's your job as the junior, lowest-ranking member, most expendable of the team. To be our hero. If you die soon after clearing your gear, we'll leave ours on and find a new spot. Testing only finds known contaminants. They develop new ones every day."

He made rank pretty quickly after that.

The DAME was fun. It was composed of me and a Major. That was it. We got to manage air corridors for the entire area that the Battalion was occupying.

No-fly zones, friend and foe corridors. If it could fly, we told it where it wouldn't get shot down at. At least not by friendly fire. Annual training was a blast in that element. Just the two of us. Scheduled classes. We got to see our aircraft make actual flights through the areas we mapped. It was all good. During war games, we got to test how our mapping and corridors worked. We'd have a red team aircraft fly outside the "safe" corridor and see how many of our units in the area called it in, tracked it, and did a mock firing at it. For the most part, we never "shot down" any friendly aircraft and tested our "Identify Friend or Foe" equipment regularly. It was good to find it worked as it should.

My final, most rewarding job was Squad leader of a Chaparral ADA Tracked Missile System while serving in Battery C (Charlie) in Artesia, NM. I had such a great crew.

Not pretty, but functional

To the point that my squad and I won *Top Gun* one year, even beating out regular army squads for the honor during annual training in 1991,

We were the first ever National Guard to be allowed to fire at night on the Missile range.

It was quite a rush, shooting down a twenty thousand dollar drone, with a forty thousand dollar missile at night. Best fireworks show, EVER.

We Took All the Awards at Annual Training 1991

I served a total of thirteen years in the National Guard. One week end a month and two weeks full time a year, with several short-term deployments to other parts of the world, and within the state of New Mexico and Texas.

Camouflage Time

We camouflaged our unit so well one day out in the field that our Lieutenant walked past us five times looking for us. We finally took pity on him and walked out and said, "Hi Lieutenant, looking for us?" It scared him half to death. We won the Camouflage competition that year.

The National Guard took a lot of work and continued education, much like the Navy and the Fire Department. Once again, I was in a "not so safe" job that had technology that changed daily and the challenges of keeping up with it.

After the Chapparal went into the history books, we picked up the Avenger system, which I liked better. It was more fun, less setup time, much like the old M42 Duster; you could "shoot on the run." An advantage over the Chaparral, which had a twenty minute setup time. (My crew could do it in eight minutes) But like I said, we had to work within our limitations. It's why technology changes daily, to overcome those limitations.

It was a simple system. Just stinger missile pods, mounted on top of a Humvee. I retired from the guard before getting to take the system to annual training, but it had HUGE potential.

It struck me as strange how we could all be so good with all this technology and yet enjoy digging foxholes and battle trenches at the same time. We always made the best of where we were and with what we had to work with. Such is life.

The total of time in the Navy and National Guard, gave me the twenty years I needed for military retirement. Both gave me my ability to do what God had planned for my future. Mainly patience, and an ability to adapt to any or no sleeping schedule, as needed. Two of the handiest skillsets needed for a long-term Alzheimer's caregiver. There is no "down time" when it comes to caring for an advanced Alzheimer's victim. They will keep you on your toes, twenty-four/seven. You either keep up with them, or get left behind and have to pick up after them, fix what they break or worse, and go look for them when they give you the slip. I managed to keep up.

Chapter 5
Clerks and Fate Meeting Rummy and Delfina for the First Time at Valley Grocery

I was twenty-eight when I met Rummy and Delfina. I had no idea how significant that Valley Grocery and the little town of Hagerman were going to be in my life that day. I just saw three very beautiful women and the owner of the store.

Delfina and Viola (Cliff's wife)

Delfina and Rummy Inside the Store

Fresh out of the Navy after nine years, I was still adjusting to life on land—and life in a small town that didn't involve ships, structure, or steel-gray sunrises. I'd taken a job delivering milk in Roswell, New Mexico. It was simple work, steady, and gave me time to think, while the road hummed under my tires. I wasn't looking for anything—especially not what I found.

Valley Grocery was one of my regular stops. A family-owned place with creaky floors, bags of beans and canned goods stacked to the ceiling, and a walk-in freezer that seemed about twenty degrees too ambitious for the desert heat. Clifford (Cliff) Martinez, the owner, was usually in the back, near the cooler. Always quick-witted, always ready with a joke. The kind of guy who could make you laugh, even while he was handing you a mop to clean up a broken jar of pickles.

He had the best meat market in the Valley. "Valley Grocery. Home of better meats." And his logo was true. No precut meat in his store. All fresh cut from fresh carcasses. That and his rotisserie Chickens and Butterfly pork chops kept him famous and in business.

Inside the Store. Note the Three with Glasses

Back row Delfina, Viola, Cliff, Grandma Martinez, Christina (Cliff's daughter)Bottom row: My Granddaughter Ray Anna, and Rummy

A note here; Cliff ended up being Mayor of Hagerman for twelve years. He was a popular guy. Always willing to lend a hand. He had the last store in the state that would let you just sign a ticket and pay later. He got sorely taken advantage of because of his good nature, but just said; "Oh well, people have to eat."

This intelligent, quick-witted public servant would also become a victim of Alzheimer's Disease in his later years. It seemed to run in the family. Their mother had it, Rummy and one of their aunts. I'm thankful it skipped Delfina. She got to keep all of our memories we made together until she passed. That is one of the saddest parts of Alzheimer's. Those memories are so very precious and they end up being just gone.

Mayor and Mrs. Cliff Martinez

One morning, as we stood near the freezer talking shop, I caught sight of three women up front near the register. All of them had glasses, all of them looked like they had better places to be than standing around waiting for two guys to stop talking milk crates and compressor fans.

I nudged Cliff and said, "Hey, you've got some nice-looking clerks up there."

He smirked and said, "Yeah, they are. Just stay away from the one with the glasses."

I looked again.

"All three of them have glasses, Cliff."

He laughed. "Exactly."

That's when he broke it down for me. One of the women was his wife, Viola—holding down the register like she ran the whole place, which, truthfully, she did. The other two? His sisters: Rummy and Delfina.

Now here's where things get interesting.

I actually flirted with Delfina first. She wasn't wearing a ring, and she had this spark in her eye—like she knew exactly what I was up to, but was going to let me try anyway. Rummy, on the other hand, was quieter, more reserved, and wearing a ring. So, I leaned toward the path that looked open.

For about two weeks, I flirted hard. Every delivery turned into a little performance. Delfina laughed at my dumb jokes, tossed a few back of her own. We had a rhythm. I thought I was getting somewhere. I found out later, much later, she thought I was cute and just fun to talk to. But time had passed, so I started mustering up some courage.

Then I finally asked her out. Nothing fancy, I said. Just lunch or dinner? A Movie, maybe? A walk?

"I can't go out with you," she said.

I blinked. "Why not?"

"I'm married. I've got six kids."

My heart sank. "But I love kids, and you're not wearing a ring."

"I never wear it at work," she said. "I'd lose it, handling all the produce and canned goods."

She paused, gave me a half-smile. "But my sister Rummy is a widow. She's single."

I glanced back at Rummy. "But she's wearing a ring."

Delfina laughed. "That's not a wedding ring. That's a birthstone ring—with our mother's and all her kids' stones on it." Her husband died in a car wreck, nine years ago. She could use a date or two.

I stood there like a sailor in a storm. I'd been steering toward one harbor, only to find out I was meant for another.

I won't lie—I was a little heartbroken. But I adjusted course.

And Rummy... well, once I really saw her, I never looked away again.

She was kind, thoughtful, with a strength that didn't need to announce itself. We started seeing each other. No games, just something steady and real. We dated heavily for a year, and during that time, my milk route got cancelled due to another provider winning the bidding war. I got hired on with Greyhound, which the store also served as the bus stop for, so it turned out nice. I still got to stop and visit now and then. I drove for about six months until I got my dream telephone call and got hired by the Roswell Fire Department—a job I'd retire from twenty years later. I gave Greyhound my resignation immediately. They have a terrible bump system. Someone with a day's seniority can take the route you're on in Roswell, and you get bumped to Albuquerque, running a short low-paying route with no recourse other than do it or leave. So, it was good to leave. Although, I did make some good trips and tours during that time. Rummy even snuck off with me on a few of them.

Ray Anna and Pamma. Road Trip

Happy Times

I also joined the National Guard and served thirteen more years in uniform. It felt like the right thing to do. And in hindsight, it was one of the best decisions I ever made. Because that flexibility, those retirements—they gave me something I never expected to need: the ability to stay home, full-time, and take care of the two women, who would shape the rest of my life.

But in that first year, all I knew was this: I had found someone who made the ground feel solid again after years at sea.

Someone, who saw me—not the uniform, not the stories, not the flirt.

Just me.

Me and Rummy

As Christmas time grew closer, I knew I wanted something to change. Rummy was more than just a girlfriend. I had told her I was in love with her after only four months into the relationship.

I thought if we just kept dating, we would not be doing each other justice. The fact is, I wanted to give her the perfect gift for Christmas that year. Why not give her me? Okay, that's a joke, sorta', but that's what I did. Man, the look on her face when I said, I know you're catholic and I'm divorced, but would you like to go down to the Justice of The Peace and get married? She literally jumped into my arms and said YES!!! While kissing me.

So, we went and grabbed Cliff and Delfina for witnesses on the twenty-third of December, and to the Justice of The Peace office we went. We headed back to their mother's house to break the news to her. She was shocked. She spoke very little English, but she got her point across. I heard her tell Rummy in Spanish, "Es otro gringo en la familia." Or, another white guy in the family, as Delfina's husband was a "gringo" also.

Gramma Nico, as we all called her, which is short for Nicolasa, let me know it made no difference. I was welcomed in as part of the family, and I was always treated as such. I was quickly acclimated into the mixed Mexican/Gringo culture. We had many parties and get-togethers over the years at her house, where you would hear a mix of Vicente Fernández and George Strait in the same playlist. Of course, the girls were always kind enough to interpret for me, so I didn't learn as much Spanish as I should have. But we all got along splendidly, probably because of the language barrier, as much as anything.

During our first year of marriage, Rummy mentioned she thought there was a way for us to get married in the Catholic church. I knew she felt bad about the shortcoming, so, I told her let's have the priest over for lunch and ask him. She said, we can't just do it like that! I said OK and that Sunday, I pulled him to the side after mass and invited him to lunch any day he could make it. It seems we could just do it like that.

At that lunch, I asked him about the possibilities, and he said I could petition the church to annul my first marriage, since I was married so young, and if it got approved, we could then get married by the church. So, that's what I did. It took six weeks of going to hearings with a group of priests, writing out an appeal, and explaining my first marriage, going to Catechism classes to learn about the Catholic faith, (I did not have to become Catholic, just agree to raise any future children we have as Catholic) and pay a one hundred-seventy-five-dollar fee for going through all of this. It all took six weeks.

The panel of priests did explain, but it didn't change the legal status of my first marriage or my children. They did not become illegitimate because of it, only the status as the Catholic Church saw things.

It did get approved, and the first miracle with me and Delfina happened, which was an unexpected result, as it turned out, there were things they hadn't told me about her and Dudley's marriage.

As it turns out, at that time, she and Dudley had been married by the Justice of The Piece for twenty-five years. She had asked him several times since they had eloped to get married by the Catholic church, since neither had been married before, so they could, but somehow, it just kept getting put off.

Delfina showed up at the house one day. I know the girls had been plotting this. She slowly brought up that she would like to get married by the church, but didn't know how to convince Dudley after all these years. I told her, let's make a double ceremony, he can't say no to that. He won't let me show him up.

She asked if I could talk to him at Sunday lunch. I said sure.

I'm not really shy, and I wasn't afraid of Dudley, like the girls and some of the rest of the family were. I said, "Hey, you old fart, what are you doing next Sunday? Why don't you do something nice for your wife? Make her happy and marry her in the Catholic church on the same altar as her sister? There's room up there for all of us, and she asked me to ask you. I told her to run while she has the chance, be she's not listening to me. She says she still loves you and you are the father of all six of her kids. You could make them all legitimate in the eyes of the church, finally."

He just did his little grin and said, well, hell, I guess I could. And that was that. The wedding was on and all their kids were about to become legitimate in the eyes of the church. Most were adults by now and didn't care, but Delfina did and that's what mattered the most.

The Priest couldn't have been happier. He got all the paperwork lined out and we had a double wedding at Saint Catherine's Catholic church, and a dance/dinner at Delfina's house after. The Priest even danced a few dances and drank some regular wine. The girls couldn't believe it. They were happy, I was happy, and Dudley even managed to smile a few times. Delfina did give me a BIG hug for that one. She said she just couldn't believe he actually went through with it. I told her, he has an old fart ego to protect. He couldn't let me get the better of him. So, I actually married Rummy twice. One year apart. It made both of them very happy, and that, in turn, made me very happy. It was a very memorable day.

It was an adventuresome life. With the Fire Department, National Guard, Welding, Wood cutting, grandchildren, and extended family. Rummy working at the store, driving a school bus (she had to get extenders to reach the pedals), you had to look twice to see the top of her head. She quit driving, a year after we got married, it was too stressful. And she also taught English as a Second Language (ESL) for about eight years. The United States of America gained over one hundred new citizens because of her work in the HELP program. She was very proud of that, as well she should have been. Her parents and family shared in that pride.

We had many parties and happy times at the house and over at the in-laws and of course at Delfina's. There was always music. Cliff and his accordion, which he could almost play. Delfina and Viola on their guitars, which they could really play. Sometimes, Delfina would play hymns on the piano and we'd all gather around and sing. We'd put a Mexican/Gringo harmony in the air and fake the lyrics we didn't know. I did learn several Spanish songs well enough that people could understand them. Times were good, more than not.

We Are Not Alike In Any Way

Cliff and His Accordion

When the girls would talk about how different they were, even though raised in the same house, I'd always show them this picture taken at a family gathering. Two peas in a pod. They would laugh, seeing this picture. Delfina would say, "Sure, in that one second."

I would tell her, "Yes, but that one second happens a lot."

We didn't know what lay ahead of us. But God had a plan.

Chapter 6
Falling for Rummy

When I started dating Rummy, it wasn't with fireworks or declarations. It was something quieter, slower—like a good rain after a long dry season. You don't realize how much you needed it until it soaks all the way through. And I had been through a rough, dry spell.

She was gentle, soft-spoken, the kind of person who listened more than she talked. That might sound ordinary to some, but when you've come from a world of noise—ship engines, firehouse alarms, barking orders—it feels like peace. She had this way of making you want to sit down and stay awhile. All that, and she loved coffee. You can't be dating anyone who doesn't love coffee after all that time in the Navy.

After the initial flirtation detour with Delfina, I'll admit I was nervous. But Rummy didn't hold it against me. If she had any reservations, she never let on. She smiled, welcomed me in, and we started going out on weekends—drives through the Pecos Valley, meals at quiet diners, evenings with her family, who already half-knew me from my milk route and Greyhound days.

If anything, from time to time, I would notice a pining look in Delfina's eyes. Maybe over a missed opportunity? Maybe just seeing her sister happy for the first time in years?

Rummy was a widow, and she carried that fact with dignity, not grief. She didn't wall herself off, but she didn't talk much about her late husband either—not right away. Her first husband had become a victim of his own making. He was killed in a single car accident, while drinking and driving. He was the one driving, and he took his work partner with him. He missed a curve in his hay truck and neither survived. It totally devastated her for years to come. She was pregnant at the time, and it hit her so hard, she miscarried, leaving Ramon fatherless and an only child. He became all that mattered to her; he was her only child. Her son, Ramon. Named after his father. She knew she'd never have another child. She had a deep, unwavering love for him, and I knew if I was going to be a part of her life, I had to respect that bond. Her husband's death strengthened it, like it had never been before. They leaned on each other a lot during those years, and even after I came into the picture, they still relied on that source of strength.

I didn't mind. I admired it. Everyone needs a shoulder to lean on. Now, they had another one.

Her son warmed up to me over time. He was calling me Dad before the wedding. I didn't try to take anyone's place—I just showed up, over and over again. Fixed what needed fixing, made her laugh when I could, talked to them about problems and anything that bothered them, and most importantly, I listened when I should.

That year felt like laying bricks—one solid step at a time. No shortcuts. We laughed often. I can truthfully say that we never had a cross word during the healthy years of our marriage. But mostly, we built something that felt sturdy, like it could hold up under weight.

We settled into a family lifestyle. Work, a vacation, or a simple road trip to visit her brother, Rick, in Lubbock or go watch him and his Mariachi band perform somewhere, either in Lubbock or Lincoln. He was a veteran, though he'd been an officer. An army captain, but in the Airborne, so I could talk to him. He's just an all-around good guy. I mean, anyone who jumps out of perfectly good airplanes, just to do it, is OK in my book. Geronimo!!!

Delfina, Rick (in Full Mariachi Regalia), and Rummy

I was working full-time at the fire department by then. Days were long, nights sometimes longer. I saw things that stuck with me. Fires, wrecks, lives changed in seconds. But when I came home, it was Rummy's presence that reset me. Her voice. Her calm. Her unwavering belief in who I was—even on days I doubted it myself. She did not want to hear what happened during my shift. She asked once. That was all. Just the one time, and cut me short while I was telling her about some of the runs we'd had.

Of course, the welding, wood cutting, and time with the National Guard, and, of course, flying my drone, helped keep things in balance. She would let me tell her all about those. She would even go with me on some of my wood cutting and drone flying adventures.

She even helped deliver a few cords of wood. It was cute, watching her walk across a yard with her few little sticks of wood, as I pushed a four-hundred-pound cartload full behind her. We'd get home, she'd make coffee and say, "I helped a lot today, huh?"

"Yes, dear, I'd still be there making the delivery if not for your help. The coffee was always good."

One evening, we were sitting on her porch, watching the sun fall over the dusty edges of Hagerman. She looked at me with that steady gaze and said, "You're not like anyone I've known."

I asked her what she meant.

"You're patient," she said. "Even when I give you reasons not to be. That matters."

I didn't know what to say, so I didn't. I just reached over and held her hand.

That was the moment I knew. I loved her. Not in the reckless way I'd imagined love in my younger years—but in the grown-up, bones-deep kind of way. The kind you build a life on.

We were married not long after. And from that moment on, no matter what came—good, bad, or impossible—I was hers. All in.

I didn't know then what the years ahead would bring. The diagnosis. The long goodbye. The caretaking and the heartbreak.

But I knew I'd signed up for all of it. Willingly. I don't give up and I don't back down. Especially, when it's something God has led me to do.

Because when you've been given something as rare and steady as Rummy's love, you hold on.

Even when it starts to slip away.

Chapter 7
Our Early Years

The early years with Rummy were good years. Real life, working-class, worn-hands, full-heart years.

We weren't rich. We weren't fancy. But we were solid. We had laid a strong foundation while we were dating. No grand expectations. No empty promises. We both knew where we stood with each other and it was on level ground. Hand in hand. On the same path. Headed for the same goal. A bright and shining future together.

I was working full-time at the Roswell Fire Department—long shifts, unpredictable calls, and sometimes, a weight on your shoulders you didn't talk about. On my days off, I would weld at a dairy, cut down trees and sell firewood or process it for selling. (Split it).

I was training or serving with the New Mexico Army National Guard. Thirteen more years in uniform after nine in the Navy might seem like a lot to some, but for me, it gave our family a cushion and, eventually, the ability to retire and do what mattered most—be present.

Rummy ran the house with quiet grace. She never demanded. She just did. Laundry, meals, mothering, loving—it all flowed from her like breathing. She didn't raise her voice much, but when she did, even the dog sat up straighter and we didn't even have a dog.

She was overall a happy, fun-loving person, and gave life her all. She had her priorities in life in the right order. God, church, family, work, self. She put everything else before herself, and it showed. Everyone around her loved her.

She took immense pride in her family. Ramon was growing into a man right in front of us. She never missed a school event, never let a birthday pass without some small celebration. Watching her be a mother to him was one of the things that made me fall deeper in love. I didn't just admire her. I respected her.

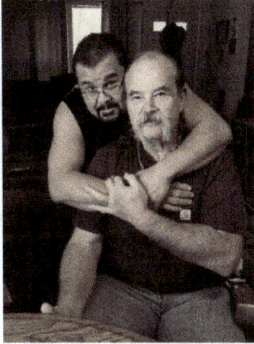

Ramon and Me

At family gatherings, I'd often find myself surrounded by in-laws speaking rapid-fire Spanish, smiling kindly, but leaving me nodding like I was two conversations behind. I spoke only a little Spanish back then—enough to get the gist but not enough to keep up. Rummy and Delfina acted as my lifeline, translating, smoothing things over with humor.

Family all Around

Rummy and Delfina Translating for their Parents

Rummy especially had a gift for it. She was a bridge between worlds—between English and Spanish, tradition and change. Her work teaching ESL with the HELP program was a reflection of that. She didn't talk much about it, but I saw the pride in her eyes when one of her students passed a citizenship test or landed a job thanks to the English that she helped them learn.

She even had me go and be the token "Gringo" many times. The students would have to talk to me in English, as my Spanish was so limited. Rummy would translate during some obvious gaps in conversation, then we'd repeat it in English. It was a fun experience for all. We made the best of things.

At home, her voice filled the space with warmth. When she laughed, it was the kind that settled into your bones. She could cook like nobody's business—enchiladas, tamales, calabacitas. Her red Chili could make you cry, and not just from the spice. It tasted like love, like a memory. Delfina was no slouch in the kitchen either, and together they had their own rhythm—recipes and stories passed between pots and pans.

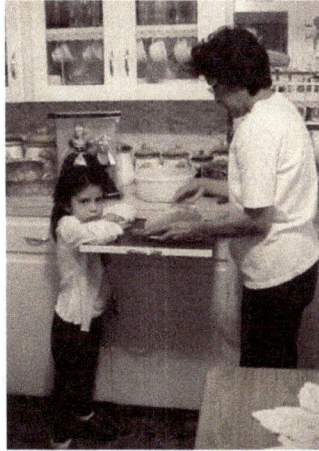

Ray Anna is Mad. Pamma Took over the Rolling Pin.

I Cooked a Small Snack for the Family

We lived simply, but it never felt lacking. A used couch could still be the setting for an evening of stories. A hand-me-down dining table could host a feast. We never needed much beyond each other and an occasional tortilla. I did learn how to cook some delicious Mexican food from both girls and still maintain their recipes in my notes. Rummy could cut up meat for her beef green Chile stew, or chicken for an enchilada casserole, by hand, and make each little cube exactly the same size. Like a machine had done it. She could cut up lettuce and tomatoes for salad the same way. I never saw anything like it, and I surely could not do it. It was fascinating to watch her do that. Her tortillas were all perfectly formed into an eight-inch circle, by hand, and I can't get them to do that, ever. Mine look like aliens, though they taste OK.

Those years were filled with purpose. Raising Ramon, working our jobs, keeping the bills paid, staying involved in church, always surrounded by the hum of extended family. I didn't realize then how much I would come to miss the sound of Rummy's voice filling up the quiet corners of the house. But miss it, I did.

But I cherished it all while I had it.

And when Ramon became a father, it felt like the circle widened again. First Arron, then Rayanna. Watching Rummy hold her grandbabies was like watching someone light up from the inside. She would hum little tunes while feeding them, whispering stories in both languages, shaping their world from the start.

We used to have such wonderful conversations. About her hometown, Hagerman, her years driving the school bus, and where we would like to go. We went to most places she named. All within the United States. We'd drive along and plan our next trip. She showed me the town she was raised in.

We'd drink coffee in the morning and watch the sun come up. We were both fortunate that way. We both loved sunrises and didn't mind getting up early enough to see them. They just made the coffee taste better. Sometimes we'd go back inside and make breakfast, or just some simple toast. We were very compatible in so many ways. When she was in her right mind, we never had a cross word. Ever.

Looking back now, those early years were golden—not because they were easy, but because they were full.

Full of meaning.

Full of love.

Full of life.

And I thank God I was there to live them with her.

Chapter 8
The First Signs

It didn't happen overnight. That's the cruel thing about Alzheimer's—it's slow. Subtle. A quiet thief.

At first, it was simple forgetfulness. A misplaced purse. A name slipping her mind. The kind of things we all do. We laughed it off, made jokes. "You're catching up to me," I'd say, trying to ease the fear neither of us wanted to name.

I don't know what's going on, she'd say. My mind just isn't thinking like it's supposed to. That was hard. To hear her acknowledge and know that she could still recognize the changes in her mind and life, and then, just as quick forget that she knew.

But then it grew. Recipes she'd cooked for decades suddenly confused her. One day she put salt instead of sugar in the empanadas. Another day she asked me how to make rice. Rummy, who used to cook with both memory and soul, couldn't follow a simple recipe anymore.

That's when I had to do something that, in her eyes, was close to betrayal—I had to take over the kitchen.

And if you know anything about traditional Mexican women, you know what that meant.

Rummy and Delfina. Waiting for Me to Finish Cooking.

For Rummy, the kitchen wasn't just a room. It was her place of power, her way of nurturing, expressing love, passing down culture, and keeping her family fed in every way that mattered. Taking that from her—even out of love and necessity—was like dimming a part of her identity.

But I had no choice.

She started leaving burners on. Forgetting ingredients. Sometimes she'd start cooking and walk away completely. I couldn't risk a fire or worse. So, I stepped in. For the last sixteen years of our marriage, I did all the cooking.

That's the hardest part to explain about Alzheimer's—how it sneaks in through the side door, quiet as a whisper, until suddenly you realize something's wrong, and worse, it's been wrong for a while.

At first, it was little things.

Rummy would forget where she'd left her keys. Then it was the stove left on, or clothes left in the washer for days. She would repeat questions, not in a frantic way, just... as if she hadn't asked them yet.

We both brushed it off at first. Who doesn't misplace things? We were getting older. Stress, long days, too much on her mind—we had excuses ready for every little slip.

But in my heart, I started noticing patterns. Small changes in her behavior. She stopped cooking as often, something that had always brought her joy. The ESL lessons she used to love? She quietly stopped taking new students. Her sentences sometimes trailed off, like the ends had gotten lost somewhere between her brain and her mouth.

One of the hardest moments came one Sunday afternoon, when we were visiting Delfina.

We were sitting in the kitchen—me, Delfina, Rummy, and Ramon. Rummy looked around the room like she didn't quite recognize where she was. Then she leaned over to me and whispered, "Whose house are we in?"

I looked at her, stunned. This was Delfina's house—her sister's house. A place she'd been to more times than I could count. The house where we'd celebrated our wedding reception, birthdays, and Christmases, where we'd laughed, cried, and danced in the kitchen. And suddenly, it was foreign to her.

I glanced at Delfina, and she saw the look on my face. Her smile faltered. That was the moment we both knew—we weren't dealing with forgetfulness anymore. Something deeper had begun.

The doctor visits came next. Tests. More questions. More blank stares.

Eventually, the diagnosis came like a slow-breaking wave: Alzheimer's.

I'll never forget sitting in that sterile white room, holding her hand as the doctor explained what was happening, what would come next, and what we should prepare for. No cure. Unreliable treatments and medications. No real signs of hope. At least we knew what to prepare for. I knew all too well from my experiences in my mom's nursing home. Rummy had the experience of dealing with her mother during her time with it. I saw the fear and anguish in her eyes.

Rummy didn't say much. She just looked at me, eyes full of something I can only describe as fear wrapped in love. I squeezed her hand and said what needed saying: "We'll face this. Together."

We'd faced so much already—loss, raising a child, the demands of service and family, life's everyday burdens. This would be no different. At least, that's what I told myself.

But deep down, I knew this was going to be the hardest chapter yet.

She was still Rummy in those early days. Still funny. Still warm. Still capable of love and comfort. But a fog had settled, and we both sensed it was only going to grow thicker.

There's no manual for watching someone you love begin to slip away—not all at once, but piece by piece. No road map for becoming a caretaker to the very person who once held your world together.

But I'd made her a promise.

And I intended to keep it.

Luckily, I had been cooking all my life, and I had paid attention to all her recipes during our marriage. I was a partner in the kitchen and had always helped with the preparation of meals, just to help take the load off her. But now, the kitchen was all mine. I was to be the head cook and bottle washer.

And not just the cooking—everything.

House cleaning. Bills. Grocery shopping. Appointments. Her medications. The long list of things we once shared became mine alone. Slowly but surely, the weight shifted onto my shoulders, and she leaned more and more on me—until one day, she didn't remember how to stand on her own. She fell once and broke her hip. Recovery was hard, as she didn't remember doing it. Then one day, during her physical therapy, which had been going so well, as the therapist and I were walking with her, gently holding her arms for balance, she lifted her legs, and we had to carry her back to the chair. She never walked again. I actually had to carry her anytime we went anywhere. Luckily, she only weighed ninety-five pounds. She never weighed more than one hundred pounds during all the time I knew her. She was tiny her whole life. But that became our life. Pick her up, set her in her wheelchair, and take her wherever we needed to go.

I never complained. Not once.

Because what we had was love. Not the Hollywood kind. The kind forged over the years. The kind that doesn't flinch when things get hard. The kind that stays when memory fades, when names disappear, and when one person has to carry both.

Rummy still smiled in those early days. Still sang softly to the radio. Still held my hand. There were good days, too—days when she seemed just like herself, even if only for a few minutes. But every day was a little different. A little more gone.

The diagnosis was just a formality. We already knew. Deep down, I think she did, too.

We faced it together, even as it took her away from me one piece at a time.

And I never stopped loving her. Not then. Not now.

Chapter 9
The Caregiver Years

People think caregiving is about medicine and memory. About keeping someone safe, making sure they're clean, fed, and dressed. And it is—those things matter. But there's another layer few talk about:

It's grieving someone who's still breathing.

Rummy was with me for 16 years after her Alzheimer's diagnosis. That's a long time to say goodbye.

At first, it was manageable. She was forgetful, but she still knew me. Still smiled when I walked in the room. We could laugh together, even if the conversation went in circles. I became the one who did the shopping, the cooking, and the laundry. Slowly, I picked up the slack she could no longer carry.

One quiet afternoon, while I was editing video in the den, a strange smell drifted in—something like oak wood smoldering. I hurried into the kitchen and found the teapot on the stove, boiled dry. Its oak handle was smoking and beginning to char. Rummy had meant to make tea, but she had forgotten and gone to take a nap. From that day on, I knew I would have to watch her more closely.

Another day, we were in the kitchen. (A lot of things seem to happen in the kitchen) She gave me what they call an "obvious indicator" of the disease. She looked at me as I was pouring coffee. We'd been married over twenty-four years by then. She asked me, "Ralph, have you ever met my father? I think he'd really like you." I had to explain, as best I could, that yes, I'd met him many times, and he just loved me.

Another time, when I was bringing her breakfast in bed, she asked me, "Sir, do you know what's happened to my family?" I explained that such as I was, I was her husband, her family.

She argued, "That can't be. I've only had one husband, and he was Mexican. I'm not even sure where he is now." All I could do was be there with her, and let her know she wasn't alone and never would be. It seemed to calm her down.

But as the disease progressed, so did the responsibilities. Rummy stopped being able to bathe herself. I had to help her dress, put on her makeup (I did find out that I'm NOT a cosmetologist), which Delfina would correct later, feed her. Remind her where we were, who I was, who she was, whose house we were in. All of the finer details of life.

She couldn't be left alone for even a minute. A stove burner forgotten, a door opened at the wrong time, a confused walk down the street—and she could be gone. I had to lock the doors. Hide car keys. Sleep with one ear open every night. I was back to my Navy days. Grabbing a two-minute catnap while standing up. Sleeping when I could, where I could. Making sure I was in a position that she couldn't get around me without waking me up. I have always been a very light sleeper. I had to be. Both aboard ship and in the Fire Department. Ready to get up and go at any time, day or night. Those sleeping habits I developed then were especially paying off for that last six years. I was down to an average of four hours a night, on a good night.

The woman I married—the strong, graceful, capable Rummy— was still there in body, but her mind drifted further away with every passing month. And yet, I never stopped seeing her. Never stopped looking for her, talking to her, holding her hand like I always had.

There were moments of beauty, even then.

One of the most heartbreaking—and somehow beautiful—things I ever witnessed was Rummy's relationship with her rag doll, April.

Rummy and April

By the later years of her Alzheimer's, she believed April was her baby. She'd rock her, feed her, give her little kisses and big hugs, sing to her, talk to her gently, and even offer her bites of food from her own plate. I never corrected her. I never took April away.

It was heartwarming and heartbreaking at the same time—watching the motherly instinct still live inside her, even when so much else had faded away. She was forever a mother. April became a very spoiled little girl.

Sometimes, I would just sit nearby with tears in my eyes, holding my breath while she brushed April's hair or whispered to her.

The day came, when even April would become just another forgotten memory. Rummy woke up one morning and didn't bother looking for April to comb her hair and get her ready for the day.

When I handed her to her, she looked confused and said, "I don't need that, thank you."

My heart just sank. I knew how April felt. It had happened to me the same way.

Love doesn't leave. It just changes shape.

Sometimes, she would hum the same lullabies that she once sang to Ramon. Or she'd squeeze my hand and smile, not quite knowing who I was but trusting that I was safe. Every once in a while, on the rarest of days, she'd look me in the eyes and say, "I love you." And I'd live off that for weeks.

But there were hard moments, too.

Sometimes, she was angry, confused, afraid. Sometimes, she cried for her mother. Sometimes, she didn't know where she was, or worse—who I was. And those were the moments that hurt the most. For the last six years of her life, she did not know who I was. I was her go-to person when she wanted something. She knew that. She'd tell Delfina, in Spanish, "Sis, if you want something to eat, let me know. I'll get the ugly, old guy that works here to fix you something. He doesn't speak Spanish, so you'll have to tell me, or tell him in English."

She would look at me with that blank stare. Knowing she should know me, but not knowing my relationship to the family, or to her.

Those moments were the hard ones.

Not because of what she said or didn't say, but because I could see the panic in her eyes—the feeling of being lost inside her own mind.

Me and Rummy, old-fashioned. She was surprised two hours later, when I showed her this picture. She had forgotten posing for it.

I cooked every meal for 16 years.

Cleaned every room.

Paid every bill.

Sat through every doctor visit and sleepless night.

I didn't do it because I had to.

I did it, because I loved her.

Love isn't just the good days. It's not just anniversaries and vacations and dancing in the kitchen. Sometimes, love is spoon-feeding someone, who once cooked every meal you ever loved. Sometimes, love is changing diapers again—only this time, for your wife. Sometimes, love is choosing not to cry, when she forgets not just your name, but who you even are, even though it breaks you inside. You continue on. Don't let on anything is wrong, because she has enough anxiety and stress, without adding any to it.

I promised her I'd stay.

And I did.

It was the hardest job I ever had. Harder than the Navy. Harder than the firehouse. Harder than anything the Guard threw at me.

But I would do it all again.

Because she would've done it for me.

Chapter 10
The Last Years

In the final years, Rummy no longer knew who I was.

That was the hardest truth to face.

She still looked at me with soft eyes, still reached out for my hand now and then—but the recognition was gone. I wasn't her husband anymore. Not in her mind. I was just a man in the room. A kind one, maybe. A safe one. But no longer the man she fell in love with, no longer the man she built a life with.

I became a stranger she trusted.

Some days, she called me by another name. Sometimes, she didn't speak at all. There were days when she would flinch if I reached to touch her shoulder, not knowing it was me. And there were days—precious, fleeting ones—when she smiled for no reason, and I could pretend, just for a moment, that somewhere deep inside, she still knew me.

But Alzheimer's is cruel. It doesn't just steal memory. It steals identity. It peels back layer after layer until only the most basic parts of a person are left—the heartbeat, the breath, the need for warmth and comfort.

So, that's what I gave her.

Warmth. Comfort. Dignity. Presence.

Even when her mind was gone, I never stopped being her husband. I changed her clothes. I brushed her hair. I talked to her every day, told her about the weather, the birds outside, what Delfina was cooking at her house across the railroad tracks. I read to her, even when she stopped understanding the words. I held her hand while she slept. I'd get her up at sunrise to go have coffee outside. I could tell she'd rather be sleeping in, but she'd sip her coffee and when she finished, I'd take her back to bed and let her sleep in. she had earned that over all the years.

I'd finish one more cup of coffee. I'd say an early morning prayer and thank God for ending the darkness with the sunrise, and ask that he do the same for Rummy. She's not in the darkness now, and for that, I'm thankful. I'm thankful that she would still occasionally have morning coffee with "the ugly, old guy that worked here."

She may not have known me.

But I knew her.

I knew the curve of her smile. I knew how she liked her socks folded. I knew that she hated the sound of thunder, but loved the smell of rain. I knew the woman she used to be, the mother she was, the teacher, the sister, the singer in the back pew at St. Catherine's. And I held all those memories for her when she couldn't anymore. That is the saddest part. Losing all those memories that you think you'll have for a lifetime.

It was around year fourteen, when her body started to decline. She could no longer walk on her own. Her appetite faded. The sparkle in her eyes dulled, like a candle burning low. By then, I was already taking care of Delfina, too. Two sisters, both needing full-time care, both leaning on the same man for everything. Delfina used to tell me what a blessing I was to both of them. I'd tell her, no, you have that backwards. You two are my double blessing. You've both given me something special in life. A true understanding of what love should really be, about what's really valuable in this life. About what really matters. And I can never, in my humble meager time left on this planet, repay God for giving it to me.

People asked me how I did it. Truth is, I didn't think about it. I just did it.

You don't count the cost when you're walking someone home, especially someone, who's so special as Rummy and Delfina. They had done so much, for so many. How could I count the cost?

I just did not. I never counted the cost at all. I could never afford the blessings they brought to me. Not ever. I only pray that I was truly worthy of such a gift.

We all have moments in our lives that are pivotal. And one day, at our house across the tracks from Delfina, I had one. A BIG one.

Since Delfina's husband, Dudley, had passed away, I had been trying my best to maintain two households, mine and Delfina's. Rummy and I would go over there on most days, and I would do projects that needed to be done. Mowing the yard, painting trim, fixing plumbing, and even welding some things out on the fence. Taking the old dog pen apart and cleaning up the area.

Delfina hadn't been diagnosed yet with Pulmonary Fibrosis, but was showing signs that something out of the ordinary was going on. She got winded during simple walks and tasks. She was always apologizing for needing to rest, and I kept telling her that it was okay, that we were just at that age.

During such a project, Delfina wanted me to go to her house and take apart some old grapevine supports that hadn't had vines in years and just looked ugly. They were having a town clean-up that day, and would come by in the afternoon to pick up whatever we put out by the curb. I already had my stuff out there, and there was plenty of time before the crew would get there.

She said she'd come sit with Rummy at our house, as Rummy had been getting very confused about which house was hers. She didn't like leaving Delfina's house to come home. She'd tell Delfina, "That man wants me to go home with him and I don't know him. I don't want to go. I want to stay here in my own house." Once I got her home, it would take some time for her to be comfortable there.

Anyway, she came over to sit with Rummy and I went and took the vine supports apart and got them out by the curb and went back to the house. Both girls were sitting side by side on the couch. Delfina started thanking me and quit, mid-sentence, and got a desperate look on her face. I could tell she couldn't breathe. I asked, "Can you breathe?" She looked at me fearfully and shook her head, "No."

I pinched her nose, tilted her head and told her; "I'm going to breath for you." I put my mouth over hers and did three rescue breaths. On the third one, she started breathing on her own again. "I don't know what happened." She said.

"I don't either," I said, "but you're going to the emergency room. That's not natural."

She tried the, "Oh, I'm okay now. I'm sure it was just a one-time thing," on me. I was very insistent and called her daughter to meet us there, with a brief explanation of what went on.

We went to the emergency room. Four hours and a bunch of X-rays later, the doctor came out and gave us the news. Pulmonary Fibrosis. I recognized the disease. As a firefighter/EMT I had run on people with it. I knew it was always terminal. My heart sank. A thousand questions from her daughter later, everyone in the room knew what I already knew. Four to six years. Once you put a time limit on life, it becomes even more precious.

That was a pivotal moment for me. I knew we couldn't waste time. I knew that I couldn't continue killing myself, going back and forth across the tracks to take care of everyone.

The next day, I made my plan known to Delfina. "You need twenty-four-hour care from now on. I need to be there to breath for you, in case it happens again." Which it did. We found out later what it was called. Lung Spasms.

I told her, "Rummy and I can move in with you. The house is big enough, we'll have our own room. I can take care of both of you, and do all the chores. You can help me with Rummy's makeup, dressing her, and other girly type things."

"But what about your house?"

I told her, "God said to sell all you have and give it to the poor. I don't need anything there. We can move what furniture you like over here. My washer and dryer are newer than yours, things like that. We'll move over to your place today, and I can deal with getting rid of things later."

"But what will the neighbors think?"

I told her, "I'm the king of 'I don't care what the neighbors think.' They should think I'm taking care of two terminally ill women, anything else is just in their minds and not really their business. We know what's going on, and that's all that matters. The ones that really know us, won't care and will be happy that you've got help. The ones that don't know us are already thinking the worst and spreading gossip about how much time I spend over her anyway, and their minds are made up, so it just doesn't matter."

Well, the Salvation Army hauled off fifty full boxes of stuff. I had a storage shed full of just stuff I hadn't looked at in years. I told them to just back their truck up to it and load what they wanted. They took that too.

I opened the house up to anyone that wanted anything and gave everything away. Clothes, dishes, furniture. Everything. In less than two weeks. One of our tiny Filipino friends, who was the same size as Rummy, came over and took most of her nicer clothes and her Merry Mushroom canister sets. Family took dishes and glasses and other stuff. When most of it was gone, some friends of mine said their daughter was looking for a house. Her husband is a real handyman and they were newlyweds. I let them move in, no money down, no set price or anything other than a prayer and a handshake. They did pay a token amount over the next couple of years, but I let them have it for less than a used car. They have since had two children and made many improvements in it. It gives me a warm and fuzzy feeling, just driving by there now. The love in the house was still there and being carried on for another family.

The three of us got settled into a survival mode and just went on about life. We made our adjustments as needed things worked out well. Delfina finally quit thinking about the neighbors and focused on how well our arrangement was benefiting us all, and what a happy little family unit we had become. Rummy was happier because she never forgot Delfina, and she had someone to protect her from the "ugly, old guy who works here." I was happy not having to hop across the railroad tracks anymore, and I was close enough that it took some stress off me for not wondering if Delfina was breathing or not. I got her a call button to wear around her neck that would ring an alarm on the one that I wore.

Between Delfina and me, our focus turned to Rummy. She had the greatest needs. I would get up and get her dressed. Delfina would do her makeup every morning and change her clothes if I had mis-coordinated them, which happened often. I would cook for us all, and life would just go on.

The final months were quiet. Peaceful, in a way. Rummy slept more. She didn't speak much. Her world had grown so small, down to a few familiar sounds and the touch of my hand. But she was safe. She was loved. And she was never alone. She never forgot who Delfina was. She always gave her a knowing smile, right up to the end.

When the end came, I was with her, and so was Delfina.

We held her hand. I told her she was beautiful. I told her I loved her, Delfina and I prayed for her and even if she didn't understand the words, I believe—I have to believe—that she felt them. That somewhere in her spirit, she knew.

Rummy passed away in 2014, after 36 years of marriage. Sixteen of those years spent slowly saying goodbye.

I didn't lose her all at once.

But I did lose her completely.

And still, I would do it all again.

Because that's what love is, in the end. Not the wedding day or the photographs or the vacations. Love is what you keep giving, long after the person you love can no longer give anything back.

That was the final gift I could give her. And I gave it with everything I had.

God called your name so gently

That only you could hear.

No one heard the footsteps

Of the angel drawing near.

Softly from the shadows

There came a gentle call

You closed your eyes

And went to sleep.

You quietly left us all......

Author Unknown.

Chapter 11
Delfina

Delfina and I had always been close. For decades, we were in-laws, friends, and co-conspirators in the family kitchen. We shared jokes, stories, music—and, eventually, caregiving. But after Rummy passed, something changed.

I'm asked sometimes, what about Delfina's kids? Why didn't they step in? The answer is simple. God didn't want them to. They all had lives, jobs, and families of their own that needed their attention. Well, that and the fact that Delfina was adamant about staying in her house. "I've lived here too long. I want to die here in my house, not in a strange place. Not even in one of my children's homes. I want to die here, in your arms." When the time came, that's exactly how she went. In her own home, with me holding her. I had promised her, as long as I was alive, she'd not go anywhere but her own home. I kept that promise. Thank God I was able to keep that promise.

Something opened.

We had both lost someone irreplaceable—she, a sister; I, a wife. But the truth is, Delfina and I had already been leaning on each other long before the funeral. We had spent years in the trenches together, caring for Rummy, trading responsibilities, late-night check-ins, small reassurances: She's okay for now. I'll sit with her. Go get some sleep. I no longer had to lean on the bulkhead while standing for my catnaps. That was actually hard to get used to.

By the time Rummy's journey ended, Delfina and I had developed a quiet rhythm. We understood each other in ways words didn't need to explain. There was no awkwardness, no guilt—only shared history, shared pain, and yes, something else growing quietly beneath the surface:

A love built not on spark, but on time.

There were two moments that sealed the bond between Delfina and me—not just as friends or in-laws, but as two people who truly understood the weight the other carried. Moments that bond you, heart and soul. A spirituality that lasts a lifetime, even if left unspoken. We both knew our moments and what they were.

The first came in 2005.

Her son Larry was murdered in his home in Roswell—shot to death by someone who had no idea the kind of light they had just taken from this world. It happened on May 5th—Cinco de Mayo—and that day would never mean celebration again for our family. Instead, it took the sunlight and dimmed this day of celebration forever in our hearts.

I still remember the silence in the house when she got the call. The way she clutched her rosary. The strength in her face, even while her hands trembled. Delfina was a mother first, always. And losing Larry—her Larry—left a wound that would never truly heal. I remember her crying, sobbing until she had to gasp for breath while I gave her a hug of consolation and a shoulder to cry on. "Oh, Ralph, my baby is gone! How could this happen? Why?"

How and why indeed. Questions that remain unanswered to this day. There is no how and why in mindless violence. Only it happened, and dealing with the aftermath.

When it came time for the trial, I stood up in court and spoke for the family. I wanted Larry's killer to know who he had taken. To know the kindness, the humor, the music, the depth of soul that had been stolen from the world that night.

Afterward, Delfina cried on my shoulder. Not just for her son, but because she knew I had taken on her pain as if it were my own. And I had. I had grown to love her children as family. Not just extended family. But my family. I was Uncle Ralph. And it is one of the best titles I've ever worn. She leaned into me after I spoke and hugged me, still sobbing, gently. I had helped her deal with her loss and pain. Given her an arm to lean on and a shoulder to cry on.

And years later, she would do the same for me.

These are the words I said to Larry's killers in court. A copy was ordered given to each of them.

Friday, January 20th, 2006

My name is Ralph Green.

I have been Larry's uncle by marriage for twenty-four years.

His mother is my wife's sister.

I'd like to say that for what you have done, I forgive you. I forgive you because I will not allow hate, anger, and irrational emotions to rule my life because of your actions.

Having said that, even though I forgive you, I will not forget it. None of us can stop that which you have set into motion.

I love Larry Stefhon. I worked with him, tried to give him advice on how to change his life for the better, and debated with him about his plans for the future. I've had Thanksgivings, Christmases, Birthdays, and many other family functions and holidays with him over the years, at his parents' house.

I, we, his family, will dearly miss him during those times in the future.

I'm a retired Firefighter. I retired from the City of Roswell Fire Department in 1999, after twenty years with the department.

During that time, it was my job to intervene on other people's tragedy. I came to realize very quickly, that I couldn't always make things better, but I could, at times, keep them from getting any worse.

That same realization is punctuated by Larry's death. It is never going to feel any better, but we are all trying, as a family, to keep it from getting any worse.

I have been on scenes, such as the one you set at Larry's house, many times.

The circumstances that brought them about made no sense to me then, and what you have done makes no sense to me now.

I know the violence and the trauma of Larry's last moments on earth, as I have lived it each time I went on such scenes, when my best efforts and those of my crew could not undo what had been done in a senseless moment of violence.

At this point, even though I and the rest of the family think your sentence is too light, I would like to thank the court for working toward a plea agreement with you, because in doing so, the family has been spared the agony, the waiting and the pain of enduring a trial, which would only have served making them relive Larry's death, all over again.

I know this court to be honorable, and I have faith that the agreement it has made was the best that could have been made, given the evidence presented to it. I trust that the sentence set forth was in the best interest of all parties involved.

As for the defendants in this case, I hope they take this time and the rest of their sentences to think of what they have done, not only to Larry and his family, but also to their own families.

You have sentenced Larry's parents and family to a lifetime of grief.

Every family function, Christmas, Thanksgiving, Birthdays, and all of the other functions, will have an empty chair at them. The joy of these events will be dampened by the absence of our beloved Larry.

You will have time to make changes in your lives. Larry's stopped where it was, and no changes can be made.

He wasn't perfect. But he was loved by his entire family.

He was about to get his driver's license back, just in time to drive his daughter to and from her high school graduation, which now, he'll never see.

He has a new nephew, his brother's son, whom he'll never get to know.

His children are left to grow up without a father. His Mother and Father no longer have the pleasure of his visits.

His brothers and sisters have only a place in the cemetery to visit with a cold stone to talk to while they're there.

Your own family's lives will be forever changed, also, because of your actions and your reckless disregard for the lives of those around you.

You don't know how many weddings, funerals, or other family functions you'll miss while in prison.

Larry will miss all of them, from now on.

What you did was the act of a coward. It was no accident. You planned it, you came at night, with weapons, the way all cowards do.

Your family will have to live with the knowledge that because of your cowardly acts, they too must suffer along with our family.

You destroyed your own lives along with Larry's. The difference is that you still have a life to try to salvage.

You have forever changed the lives of so many people you don't know, in such a way that we'll never fully recover from the loss.

There is little satisfaction in knowing you won't either.

You have limited your future by your own actions, but you have ended Larry's future and any hopes his family had for him.

Take time to think of what value you place on a human life, and of what your lack of any real human values have cost you, your family, and the family and loved ones of Larry.

You're going to have plenty of time to think.

I truly hope you make good use of it and use it for good.

That's all I have to say,

I thank the court for its time

Ralph Green (AKA: jafff)

View Larry's Memorial Video Here:

On January 24th, 2013, Delfina's husband of 57 years passed away. His name was Dudley. I won't speak ill of the dead, but I will say that his absence did not leave the same kind of quiet as his presence had. Despite a few faults, like we all have, he was a good and trusted friend. Overall, he was a good provider for his family. A hard worker who had more good in him than bad. He did fifteen years in the Air Force and eight years in the Army Reserve. His time in service is an honor to his legacy.

A week later, on January 31st, we were returning to Delfina's house after his funeral. We were gathering for the family meal, still heavy with grief, trying to steady ourselves again. We were making preparations for the family meal. The entire family was there and grieving. That's when my phone rang. I was in no way prepared for this call.

It was my son Allen, so I initially smiled and answered with, "Hello there, son. How're you doing?"

He didn't even say hello or give a greeting in return.

"Is Troy with you?" he asked.

"No," I said. "Was he coming down?"

"He's missing."

"Missing? From where?" I asked.

Allen continued, "He told his wife he had a five-day work conference in Denver, starting Friday. He left Thursday night, and she hasn't heard from him since. He's not answering his phone, and his boss says it was only a one-day conference on Friday, and that Troy never showed up for it."

She had tried to find him by seeing if he'd used his debit card, which he did at a sporting good shop near the Bear Lake facility in the Rocky Mountain National Park.

They were hoping that he'd made a detour and come to see me.

That was not the case. Allen said they would keep looking and that he was going to meet Troy's wife there at the store later that day, and he would keep me posted.

Then came the hard part. The waiting. The not knowing. The constant wondering and prayers. Wanting the phone to ring, but wanting it to remain silent at the same time.

Then came the call.

The update would not be good news. Troy had not taken a walk about. He hadn't met someone and run off with her. No good case scenario. A parent's worst nightmare had come to pass.

My heart dropped. Troy was my youngest. A beautiful, sensitive soul. He had struggled for years with PTSD after his service and time in Afghanistan. He had survivor's guilt. He was a plumber in the Air Force. Always the first ones in to a new area to set up water supply and purification. He had been working in a ditch when EOD set off an IED they had discovered. It collapsed the ditch he was in. He was at the shallow end. It broke both his ankles, but he had two teammates working in the other end, the deep end. They were both buried alive and died horrible deaths, suffocated by the dirt they were trapped under before anyone could get to them. I had talked to him about it and explained every time, it just wasn't his fault and it wasn't his time to go. Still, his guilt persisted until he buried it in that dark place, we put the things we don't want to think about. But they always find a way to creep back up to the surface. Sometimes, bursting out of that space with a vengeance, and seem worse than when they actually happened. If you push it back in and don't cope with it, it becomes the monster that it is.

I worried about him, especially, when he quit talking about things. His wife had told him not to bother others with his problems. I prayed for him. Prayed with him. Prayed even more when he went missing. And now, he was gone. I had such a terrible feeling in my heart and prayed it wouldn't come to reality. But it did.

Five days passed before they found his body in the Bear Lake area of Rocky Mountain National Park. He had taken his own life.

Troy at this time had finished college. He was an electrical engineer and a computer whiz. He wrote code and algorithms.

He had a six-figure income, a beautiful home in a gated community. No financial problems, things at home seemed normal, wonderful even.

He believed in redundant systems. Failure was never an option. He went there to do what he did.

He had a redundant plan, even for his death. He'd stabbed his arm, seven times. Trying to hit the radial artery which he knew was there. No, he didn't miss it. Part of his redundant plan worked against him. It was thirty-five degrees below zero Fahrenheit that day. The extreme cold actually restricted the bleeding. Each stab wound immediately closing up, due to the cold and minimizing the bleeding.

Plan B.

He'd bought a short lanyard at the sporting store. He tied it to a low hanging branch, formed a noose around his neck and leaned into it, until he passed out, thus hanging himself.

Three redundant methods. If the stabbing and hanging didn't work, the overnight in the subzero weather surely would. It was just his way of thinking. He had lied about his whereabouts to insure he wouldn't be found in time. And he wasn't.

The cold was so severe that his body had to be thawed for three days before they could perform the autopsy.

A couple hiking the seldom used snowshoe trail saw a man standing in front of a tree over one hundred yards off the trail. Just standing. They shouted and asked if he was okay. Getting no response, they moved closer.

Horrified by what they found, they notified the authorities. The search for my son had ended in a horrible tragedy.

LOCAL

Body Of Missing Hiker From Texas Found Near Bear Lake

February 5, 2013 9:43 PM

ROCKY MOUNTAIN NATIONAL PARK, Colo. (CBS4) – Rocky Mountain National Park officials believe they have located the body of a man who went missing in the park.

Crews had been searching for Troy Green, 39, in the Bear Lake area since Friday. The area has received about nine inches of snow since last Wednesday.

Tuesday afternoon two people who were snowshoeing north and west of Bear Lake told

The grief nearly swallowed me. I had never had such a horrible pain that just seemed to be squeezing the breath and life out of me. I had Rummy to take care of and she just didn't understand why the guy who worked here was crying. I tried not to do that in front of her, but I have to admit, I just couldn't keep from it sometimes. She would ask me are you feeling bad, sir? It only multiplied the pain. I could not share my grief with my wife of so many years. She had forgotten both my sons by now, and explaining what happened only served to confuse her more. Delfina ran interference with her and tried to shield her from any of the trauma.

I couldn't breathe properly for weeks. I couldn't think straight. I traveled to San Antonio for his memorial, as Troy was cremated, and when I returned, it was Delfina who was waiting for me at the door. Her arms open for a soothing, badly needed hug. I could never really imagine her pain of losing Larry. No one who hasn't lost a child can ever imagine that pain. Now, I had a complete understanding of her feelings. The anguish, the emptiness in her heart that had been there since that day. I could truly empathize with her now. We had that "common point of reference" Spock had spoken of.

She had watched Rummy while I was gone. But more than that— she had held space for my grief the same way I had held space for hers.

And now, it was my turn to cry on her shoulder, and cry I did. She'd never seen me cry before, but during her soothing hug, she saw it and helped me through it. Again, the "How and the why" would remain unanswered. It would take me nine years, before I could bare to see Troy's name chiseled in stone. His wife kept his ashes, so there could be no memorial jewelry made from the as a small remembrance of him for me. I decided I wanted a bench, here in the local cemetery. A place, where I could go sit and talk to him while sipping coffee and praying. I just couldn't bring myself to do it, so it got put off. Then, one day in 2022, I woke up a little bit. If I didn't buy the bench, it just wouldn't get done. I had to have something with Troy's name on it to go visit. I looked at different benches and through my tears, ordered the one featured in "About the author."

When Troy was found, and we had to get back into our daily routines, we just went about our daily duties and did what needed to be done.

We both had lives that needed attention. She'd just lost her husband of fifty-six years and had to deal with a huge cut in her income and now the responsibility of the total household was hers alone.

We didn't need to say much. Just being there for each other was enough. Sometimes, we sat in silence. Sometimes, we told stories about our boys. Sometimes, we just held each other, letting the ache pass between us like prayer beads slipping slowly through the fingers of time.

We both knew what it was like to lose a child.

We both knew what it was like to feel a part of yourself go with them.

A parent is just not supposed to outlive their children.

That kind of grief either breaks people apart or binds them together.

For us, it was the latter.

***

After Rummy passed away, with only the two of us left, we both asked, "What now?"

Delfina still needed a caregiver. I still needed a place to live as I had literally given everything away to free me up to care for the two of them.

But what now? We were far beyond, "What will everyone say and think?" We were in survival mode.

Delfina's condition had only gotten worse. Moving out and leaving her to fend for herself was not an option to even consider. The yard needed care. Cooking needed to be done. The housework wasn't going to do itself.

The decision made itself. Let the whispers begin. We were living in reality. We didn't have the luxury of time to figure things out, or care what anyone would say. We both knew that life had to go on and that meant me remaining as her companion and caregiver.

We didn't rush into anything. How could we? We were still grieving. Still adjusting to silence, where once there had been Rummy's voice. But grief has a way of clarifying what matters. And I began to see Delfina differently—not as my sister-in-law, but as someone who had been standing beside me all along, through the best and worst parts of my life.

She had always been strong, but there was fragility now, too. In 2013—the same year her husband of 56 years passed—Delfina was diagnosed with pulmonary fibrosis. The doctors said it was terminal. She never let it stop her from caring for Rummy, never let it show. But I saw it.

90

I saw how she sat a little longer at the table. How the oxygen tube became a permanent fixture. How walking across the room left her breathless. And I saw how she still smiled through it all.

I started doing more for her—quiet things at first. Groceries. Driving. Cooking her favorite meals. She resisted, at first. Delfina was proud, just like her sister. But pride softened into partnership. And somewhere along the way, partnership became something more.

We were two people who had lost so much.

But we still had each other.

When I asked her to marry me, it wasn't with grand speeches or fireworks. It was simple. Honest. We've already built a life together. Let's make it official.

And she said yes.

In 2015, Delfina and I were married. Not in a big ceremony. We wanted to make it moral within the church, not necessarily legal in the eyes of man. She had benefits she needed to keep. Insurance and the like. We found a sympathetic and accommodating Catholic Priest in Denver during one of our trips. We went to the cathedral in St. Joseph's Hospital with him and two nurses. He married us in the eyes of the church, something our local priest had reservations about doing, but not this priest. He was truly a man of God.

Some people were surprised. Some didn't understand. But we didn't need their understanding. We had our truth. We had 40 years of friendship, of shared memories, of faith and family and laughter and tears. What we had wasn't a replacement for what came before—it was a continuation of love, in a new form.

We made each other happy.

We teased each other. We sang together—she still had a beautiful voice, even with weakened lungs. She played her guitar when she had the strength. I cooked her favorite meals. She corrected my Spanish; I made her laugh with my stubborn English. We made the most of every day, knowing we didn't have forever.

Because we never do.

Chapter 12
Breathing Time

Delfina's illness had already begun its quiet intrusion before we married. Pulmonary fibrosis is a thief. It doesn't make a lot of noise—it just takes. Little by little. Breath by breath.

She had been diagnosed in 2013, the same year she lost both her husband and my son Troy. Maybe it was all too much. Maybe the body has limits when the heart has carried too many losses.

But if Delfina ever felt sorry for herself, she never showed it. She adjusted. Slowed down. Used her oxygen. Made jokes. She was always stubborn about dignity. She didn't want to be a burden.

She never was.

When we got married in 2015, we both knew we weren't promised decades. We were promised days. Moments. But we also knew what to do with those.

We made them count.

I cooked for her. Did the laundry. Took care of her medications, her appointments, and her comfort. She could no longer stand for long, and sometimes even walking from the couch to the bathroom wore her out. She'd pause to catch her breath, embarrassed, but I never let her feel shame.

I told her, "You've spent your whole life serving others. Let someone take care of you for a while."

Still, she tried to keep her routines. She read. She watched her shows. She prayed, always. And sometimes, she still played her guitar—hands trembling, voice soft—but when she sang, it felt like time stopped. I loved her beautiful voice and would often sing with her, such as in the "Libro Abierto" video. The last time she had the energy to play her guitar and sing.

One special moment was, when I decided to take away some of her anxiety and stress. When Dudley passed, her income was literally cut in half. She lost his City of Roswell retirement due to the option he had chosen. His military and Social Security remained, but it was a huge financial setback, as they had bought a new car, shortly before his passing and the payments were a good chunk of her income. She never asked for help, but I had told her, "I have two vehicles here. We really don't need yours. You can't drive anymore, and I do all of it. Let's get rid of your car."

Well, we found out that wasn't an option. She owed more than it was worth, naturally. I was asking her little personal questions. Who was the loan through? Interest rates, etc. Small things, so she couldn't catch on. She had formulated a plan to give her car to her granddaughter and let her son make the payments. I told her that was a good idea, only if he could put the car in his name, which I knew couldn't happen for reasons I knew, that she didn't. He, of course, was all for it but wanted to leave it in her name. I told her she would end up making the payments if that happened, as I knew he couldn't really afford it, for reasons I won't disclose.

A week later I told her it's okay to give your granddaughter the car now. She asked, "What's different?"

I told her, "Well, the car is paid off and I just got the title in the mail."

She did her, "Surely you're not serious?"

And I did my, "I am serious. And don't call me Shirley" line.

"I can't afford to pay off the car in a lump sum."

"You don't have too. It's already done." She cried and called her son, who even though he agreed on the payments, never made one and I knew before she talked to him, he couldn't make them.

94

So, no disappointments. Only love shared. All was good with God and the world. I just wrote it off with the rest of his "loans." His mother need not have any more stress in her life. And I feel blessed having been able to relieve part of it.

We didn't talk much about the end. We didn't need to. It lingered quietly between us, like a shadow at the edge of the room. But what mattered more was the light. The life. The love.

Some days, I'd catch her looking at old photographs—her kids, Rummy, her choir friends from St. Catherine's. She'd say things like, "I wonder what Heaven smells like." Then she'd smile. Not afraid. Just curious. I told her, "It's not nearly as beautiful as it will be when you get there." She'd smile. "I wonder if I can sing in their choir?" and "I hope I can touch Jesus's hand when the time comes." I'm sure she got to.

Her faith never wavered.

Her body, though, did. Slowly. Deliberately. Like a house with creaking beams, giving way one day at a time.

By 2018, we were mostly homebound. I'd wheel her out into the sun when I could. Sometimes she'd nap in her chair with her smart phone playing soft Spanish hymns. I'd sit nearby, just listening to her breathe.

Or not breathe.

Every cough was a reminder. Every pause. Every sharp intake of air. She was slipping, and I couldn't stop it. I had been here before—with Rummy. I knew the look in the eyes. The weariness in the shoulders. The silence that wasn't just tiredness, but surrender.

Still, Delfina never complained. Even as her oxygen levels dropped. Even when every breath came with effort. Even when she knew the end was close. She was the bravest, most fearless person I've ever known. "I've no reason to fear. God gave me so much love through my children and you. I have no regrets."

She'd say, "We've had a good run, haven't we?"

"Yes ma'am. We surely have. It's been a wonderful run." Because we did have a wonderful run.

We had love that bloomed late, but burned bright.

We had mornings filled with coffee and music.

We had shared grief that somehow grew into shared peace.

But her oxygen levels began to drop, daily. She did not want to be resuscitated. She had made that clear. "I want to hold hands with Jesus as I pass over and I don't want to be interrupted."

The day we knew was coming, finally had a sunrise. As the sun escaped the darkness, Delfina went to bring her light and love to heaven.

Delfina passed in 2019, in the home we shared, in the arms of someone who loved her without condition. One last kiss goodbye as she slipped into her final coma. She left this world as gently as she lived in it—quiet, proud, faithful. I feel especially blessed to have her in my life for as long as I did. I was there as she wished. I said my goodbyes and she simply took the hand of Jesus and left us all here. The way she said she wanted to go.

In her own house, and me holding her in her arms.

And I've missed her every day since.

Chapter 13
Little Things, Big Love

You learn pretty quickly when you're caring for someone with a terminal illness that love doesn't live in the grand gestures—it hides in the small things. A warmed blanket. A spoonful of broth. The way you hold a hand just a few seconds longer because you know it might be one of the last times.

That's how it was with Delfina and me.

We had routines. Sacred little rituals that filled the spaces between doctor visits and oxygen refills.

Every morning, I'd fix her coffee. Not too strong, not too sweet—just how she liked it. She'd be sitting at the table with her nasal cannula hissing softly, the concentrator running not so quietly in the background, flipping through the church bulletin or crossword puzzle. Sometimes, she'd hum a tune from her choir days, and I'd stop what I was doing just to listen.

She still had her sense of humor. Sharp as ever.

Once, I walked into the room with a towel wrapped around my waist after a shower, and she looked at me over the top of her glasses and said, "Put some pants on before you scare the angels away."

We laughed for ten minutes.

Another time, I burned the beans—bad—and she teased me for a week. "You're lucky I can't stand long enough to cook," she said, "or I'd make you eat your own tortilla disasters." And then she kissed my cheek.

When you know time is short, even arguments become precious. There was the Great Pillow War of 2016—she insisted on the flat one, I wanted her to have more support. We compromised: one flat, one fluffy. She won, of course. Delfina always won.

Evenings were our softest hours.

I'd make dinner—something light, usually—and we'd eat together at the small table, hands touching. We'd watch reruns of Bonanza or Sabado Gigante, depending on her mood. Sometimes we'd sit in silence, letting the day end slowly.

And on special nights, she'd let me dance with her.

Not a real dance. Not like before. But I'd lift her gently, oxygen tube and all, and sway with her just a little, right there in the living room. Her cheek against my chest. My hand in hers. A song playing low on the radio. Maybe something by Vicente Fernández, or Vern Gosden. Maybe just the sound of the ceiling fan.

I would even lift her up into my arms, when she got too weak to stand. Just to share the moments I knew she love.

Those moments didn't last long. Her lungs couldn't take it. But she'd smile up at me afterward like we'd just been on a ballroom floor somewhere in Heaven.

"This," she'd whisper, "is enough."

And it was.

It was everything.

We weren't just two people waiting for the end. We were two souls wringing every drop of sweetness from what time we had. Love in the quiet. Love in the exhaustion. Love in the deepest ache of knowing tomorrow might be worse than today—but still choosing to show up.

Still choosing each other.

Always.

Chapter 14
The Mile-High Honeymooners

Pulmonary fibrosis doesn't negotiate—but we did. We refused to let it take everything at once. Instead, we took what it gave and made the most of it.

That's how our monthly trips to Denver started.

National Jewish Health Center and St. Joseph's Hospital were the only ones willing to treat Delfina. Nobody in New Mexico or Texas wanted to touch her case—not with her lungs the way they were. But in Denver, there was still hope. And where there was hope, we went.

We'd pack like we were going on vacation—and in many ways, we were. We turned those medical trips into mini-honeymoons. Ate in little diners along the way. Laughed in hotel rooms. Snuck moments of normal in between oxygen tanks and clinical visits.

It gave us something to look forward to—something to plan for. Something that wasn't just about dying.

One trip, though, didn't go as planned.

Her right lung collapsed without warning.

We were life-flighted to Denver on a turboprop. The engine roared like a beast, but all I could hear was my own heart pounding. I was terrified. But I couldn't show it. I had to be steady. For her.

She clutched my hand as we lifted off. "I guess, if we go down, we'll go down together," she said, and smiled weakly.

Even then, she had that quiet grace.

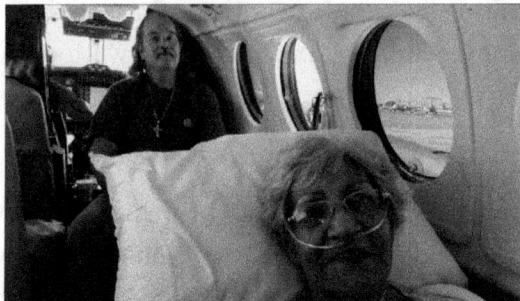

I was in the middle of remodeling our master bathroom, when it happened. Had it torn down to the studs. Pipes exposed. Tile ripped up. I had planned it with her in mind—grab bars, a walk-in shower, a seat, everything. I just didn't expect to be away from it for three weeks. It stayed in pieces until we got back.

The Original Pink Tile

The Demolition Begins

More Demolition

While we were in Denver, she said to me, "I guess, I'll have to see it from Heaven when you finish it."

I held her hand and said, "No. Jesus is going to let you see it in person. And you're going to use that shower. You're going to lean on those handrails and tell me I missed a spot on the grout."

And she did.

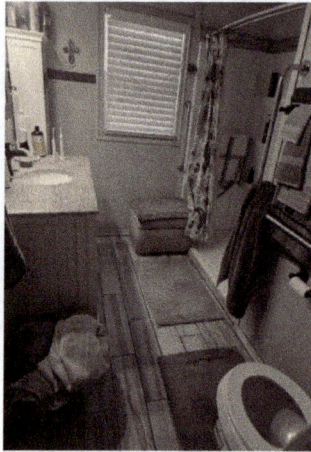

10 Days After We Got Back

Three more years. Three more beautiful, ordinary, holy years.

She saw the finished bathroom. Showered in it. Laughed when I installed the towel bar crooked and fixed it twice. She got those extra years because of the care we fought for—and the care we gave each other.

She was the strongest, most righteous person I've ever met. Her faith never cracked. Her spirit never broke. And her joy never dimmed.

Even in the worst of days, she'd light up when I walked into a room. I used to tell her, "I hate to compare you to a dog, but you're like a puppy. You know how happy a puppy looks when they see you? That's the look you give me—every time I bring you a cup of coffee."

She'd laugh. Not because it was such a funny line, but because it was true. Her eyes sparkled like she'd been waiting all day just for me to show up.

I'll never forget the first time I brought her breakfast in bed.

She cried.

Through her tears, she said, "Dudley never brought me even a glass of water in all our years together. You tell me I'm beautiful and that you love me more times in the first hour we're awake than he did in our entire marriage."

Then she said the words that I carry like a medal in my heart.

"You're such a good man."

I had done many things in my life—served in the Navy, fought fires, raised children, faced heartbreak—but that moment was something else. To be seen. To be known. And to be called good by the woman you love?

That's what you live for.

Chapter 15
Borrowed Time, Blessed Time

Borrowed time is still time—and we made it holy.

Those last three years after her lung collapsed felt like a gift wrapped in miracle paper. Not because every day was easy, but because every day was ours. The clock was ticking, sure—but we refused to live by the sound of it.

We lived by the smell of fresh tortillas, the hum of Sunday morning Mass on TV, the soft clink of her rosary beads, and the shuffle of my feet in the kitchen, trying to remember her chili recipe without getting scolded from across the room.

She couldn't be on her feet long, but that didn't stop her from being in charge.

"Not too much cumin," she'd call out. "And stir with love, not frustration!"

I told her once that if she ever left me a recipe book, I hoped it came with commentary. She said, "You don't need a book. You've been cooking with your ears."

She still had her guitar then. Not always the strength to hold it long, but every now and then, she'd pluck a few chords. Sometimes, I'd catch her playing "Amor Eterno" softly, when she thought I wasn't listening. I'd sit nearby and not say a word. Just let the music settle in the space between us like incense.

We had visitors often—kids, grandkids, nieces, nephews. Everyone loved being around her. She had this magnetism. Quiet, but powerful. She could settle a room with a word. And she never stopped being a mother, or a sister, or a tía.

Sometimes, she'd watch them laugh and play, and I'd see a tear run down her cheek. Not out of sadness, just gratitude. "God has been good to me," she'd whisper. "Better than I deserved."

I never agreed with that last part.

She deserved every blessing that came her way. And I reminded her, often.

Our bed became her throne in those later years. I brought her breakfast most mornings—oatmeal with cinnamon, or toast with a thin layer of butter and honey. She'd grin at me like I was bringing her room service at the Ritz.

"You spoil me," she'd say.

"You're easy to spoil," I'd answer.

Sometimes, we'd just sit in bed together, reading or listening to soft music. My arm around her. Her head on my shoulder. I swear, I've never felt more at peace than in those quiet, ordinary hours—when the world stopped demanding anything of us, and we could just be.

The oxygen machine hummed beside the bed like a distant lullaby. I came to know every beep, every click, and every rhythm of that thing. I hated what it meant, but I was grateful for what it gave us: more time.

She loved when I read to her. Scripture. Poetry. Even old love letters. She said my voice was soothing. Said it reminded her she wasn't alone.

And she wasn't.

Not for one moment.

Not even in the hardest hours.

We had settled into our rhythm by then—oxygen machines, doctor visits, good days and bad. But even in the middle of all that, there were small, quiet surprises that made life sweet.

Like the morning, I woke up craving sopapillas.

She was still sleeping, her breathing soft and steady beside me. I didn't want to wake her, but I couldn't get the thought out of my head—hot sopapillas, golden brown, with honey dripping down the sides.

So, I got up, real quiet, and made a full batch from scratch. Rolled out the dough just the way I remembered, fried them to puffed perfection, and had the coffee brewing, when the smell finally woke her up.

She blinked at me from bed, eyebrows raised. "Where did you get sopapillas this early in the morning?"

I smiled. "Well… we had flour and stuff."

She sat up slowly, eyeing the plate like I'd just brought her something from a restaurant in Santa Fe. She took a bite, still stunned. "Are you serious, Ralph?"

That became her signature line to me from then on. *"Are you serious, Ralph?"*

And like clockwork, I'd deadpan right back, "I am serious. And don't call me Shirley."

She'd laugh, every time. Same joke. Same delivery. It never got old. It wasn't really about the punchline—it was the joy in sharing the moment, knowing we were still surprising each other. Still learning. Still loving.

She once told me, "You're full of secrets. Quiet ones. The kind that sneak up and make a home in your heart."

That morning with the sopapillas was just flour and stuff on the surface. But to her—and to me—it was one of those tiny, holy acts that said: I love you. I see you. And I'm still going to spoil you, every chance I get.

Chapter 16
The Softening Days

Time had started to fold in on itself.

Days were slower now. More fragile. But not empty. Never empty.

Delfina's body was weakening; there was no denying that. The therapy trips to Denver had grown more difficult. The recovery periods between them stretched longer. I watched her carefully—counted her breaths without her noticing, studied the color in her face, adjusted her pillows with the tenderness of a man placing flowers at an altar.

She still smiled. Still found the strength to tease me. Still asked if I was "serious, Ralph," almost daily.

But the spark was dimming. Slowly. Like a candle protecting its last few flickers.

There were quiet changes. She started sleeping more. Her appetite faded. She stopped playing the guitar—her hands too tired, her lungs too shallow. The music that once floated through our home was now a whisper in memory.

But love was loud.

The way she looked at me when I brought her coffee. The way her hand sought mine in the dark. The way she'd rest her head against my chest and listen to my heartbeat like it was a lullaby meant just for her.

She was never afraid. That was one of the things that amazed me. Delfina had a calm about her, a deep peace. Maybe, it came from her faith. Maybe, from a lifetime of surviving hardship. Maybe, it was just who she was at her core—an unshakable soul in a fragile frame.

One day, she told me, "I don't think I'm going to make it to next Christmas."

We were sitting by the window, watching a hummingbird dance near the feeder I'd put up for her. She said it as easily as if she were commenting on the weather.

I didn't say much back. Just squeezed her hand.

She didn't need comfort. She needed presence.

So, I gave her that. Every minute I could.

I read to her more. We watched old black-and-white movies. I cooked soft foods that she could still enjoy—caldos, arroz con leche, buttery mashed potatoes. Every now and then, I'd catch her sneaking a bite of something she knew she shouldn't have.

"I thought you weren't hungry," I'd say.

"I'm not," she'd reply, "but that doesn't mean I don't want it."

That was Delfina. Honest, funny, and still full of life, even when her body was letting go of it.

One evening, after a particularly rough day, she looked at me for a long time before speaking.

"You know what makes me sad?" she asked. "That I won't be here to see you finally rest."

That broke something in me.

Because resting was never the point. Loving her—caring for her—that was the rest. That was the peace.

And in that moment, I think she knew it.

She laid her hand on my cheek and said, "I hope you know you've already given me heaven on earth."

Chapter 17
When the Light Fades

We always think we'll know when the end is near. But the truth is, it comes like fog—quiet, soft around the edges, settling in before you realize you're already standing in it.

Delfina's decline came not as a crash, but a drift. A slow loosening from the world. From her breath. From pain.

She'd already stopped singing. Stopped trying to walk across the room. I had to help her with more, but she still wanted to hold onto little pieces of independence. That was important to her.

"I'm not helpless," she'd say. "Just winded."

I smiled, and let her have that.

She never complained. Not once. Not about the tubes, the fatigue, the loss of strength. But I could see it in her eyes—she was tired. The kind of tired that sleep doesn't touch.

The oxygen concentrator became our background music, a steady hum that marked the rhythm of our days. I'd make sure her spare batteries were charged. Tuck the cannula gently behind her ears. Adjust her pillows. Sit beside her and read, or just hold her hand.

Sometimes, we didn't say much.

Sometimes, that silence was the conversation.

Her family came by more often. So did mine. Everyone wanted to sit with her, touch her hand, kiss her forehead. She accepted it all with grace, never wanting to make anyone sad—even as she faded.

She loved her Grandchildren

One evening, she asked me to read her favorite Psalm.

"The Lord is my shepherd; I shall not want…"

Her lips moved with mine, almost soundlessly.

She smiled when I finished. "I like the part where He makes us lie down in green pastures. Sounds nice, doesn't it?"

"It does," I said, swallowing the lump in my throat.

She closed her eyes, and I sat with her until the sun went down.

***

The night she passed, the house was still. Even the oxygen machine seemed quieter, like it knew.

I had just brought her some warm broth. She couldn't eat, but she liked the smell of it.

She looked up at me, her eyes glassy but full of love.

"You've taken such good care of me," she whispered.

I kissed her forehead. "That's what love does."

She held my hand, and we sat in the hush together, no TV, no music. Just two souls letting go slowly.

And then... she exhaled.

And didn't breathe in again.

I didn't panic. I didn't cry right away.

I just stayed there, holding her hand. Thanking God. And telling her over and over, "You were the best thing, Delfina. The best."

***

I dressed her carefully. Brushed her hair. Lit a candle.

I made sure she left this world the way she lived in it—dignified, loved, and wrapped in peace.

Her passing didn't feel like an end. It felt like a door opened, and she finally stepped through into the green pastures she always talked about.

Chapter 18
What Love Leaves Behind

It's a strange kind of silence that follows death.

Not the peaceful kind you get in the early morning or the quiet of a church.

It's hollow. It echoes. It waits for someone who isn't coming back.

For the first time in years, there was no oxygen machine humming. No soft voice calling my name from the other room. No Delfina waiting for her morning coffee, eyes shining like I was the best thing she'd ever seen.

The stillness nearly crushed me.

I walked through the house slowly, like I didn't belong in it anymore. Her things were where she left them—her Bible, her glasses, the little shawl she kept on the recliner.

Everything looked paused. But the world didn't pause. The sun still came up. People still smiled at the grocery store. Time marched on, while my heart stayed with her.

***

Grief didn't come all at once. It leaked in.

In the scent of her lotion. In a song on the radio. In the quiet habit of turning to say something and remembering there was no one there to hear it.

I still cooked breakfast for two.

I still poured her a cup of coffee.

It took weeks, before I could stop setting her place at the table.

But in that heavy sorrow, something else was growing—gratitude.

I had been loved. Fully. Deeply. Twice in my life, in ways some people never know even once.

And I had loved just as fully in return.

That kind of love doesn't leave you. It lingers in your bones. In your breath. In your prayers.

***

People came around. Family. Friends. Neighbors.

They brought casseroles and stories. Some cried. Some just hugged me and said nothing. That meant more than words.

Ramon came and sat with me for hours. We didn't need to talk much. We just sat on the porch, remembering. Sometimes he'd share old stories about his mom—about Rummy's fierce protectiveness or her quiet way of teaching by example.

Sometimes we talked about Delfina. How she always had a song in her heart, even when life knocked the wind out of her.

***

But the moments I remember the most were the quiet ones, when I was alone and felt her presence.

Sometimes, I'd walk into a room and swear I could still smell her perfume.

Other times, I'd feel this warm stillness settle over me, like she was resting a hand on my shoulder from the other side.

She once told me, "If God lets me look in on you, you'd better not be moping."

I smile when I remember that.

Because I do mope sometimes. But I also get up. I finish the things she didn't get to see finished. I water the flowers. I make the sopapillas. I sing her songs softly, even if the words catch in my throat.

***

Love like that doesn't leave. It changes form.

It lives in the way I treat others. In the patience I show. In the care I give. In the memories I carry like sacred stones.

I still talk to her. Not out loud, but she hears me.

And when I close my eyes and think of Delfina, I don't see her sick. I see her strong. Vibrant. Smiling. Sitting at the piano in St. Catherine's choir loft, her voice rising like a prayer.

She's not gone.

She's just somewhere I can't follow—yet.

But I will.

One day.

And when I walk into that room, I already know what I'll see—

Her eyes lighting up, like a puppy's, happy I've finally come home.

Chapter 19
Delfina's Chapter

Delfina's strength was quieter than Rummy's, but it ran deep. Where Rummy had been quick to laugh, to talk, to fill the room with energy, Delfina was more reserved, letting her music and her steady hands speak for her. She had a gentleness that could ease the hardest day, and a stubborn streak that showed itself whenever someone she loved needed defending.

Her health was never perfect in the years I knew her. Breathing became a battle over time, and the oxygen tanks became her constant companions. Standing for long periods grew difficult, so her days in the kitchen grew fewer. Still, when she did cook, her meals carried the same warmth as her music—simple, nourishing, and filled with love. By then, I had taken over most of the cooking, but Delfina still guided me, offering tips, seasoning advice, and sometimes just sitting nearby to keep me company while I worked.

Our lives after Rummy's passing were shaped by routine—doctor's appointments, medications, the careful planning of each day to make sure Delfina had the strength for what mattered most. What mattered most, more often than not, was people. She lit up when family visited, when grandchildren or great-grandchildren filled the house with laughter. Even when she could no longer join in fully, she delighted in watching them, smiling from her chair with April—the doll Rummy had once adored—resting on her lap.

There were quiet moments, too, when it was just the two of us. Evenings when I would bring her tea, set her oxygen by her side, and she would hum softly—old hymns, bits of Spanish folk songs, or melodies she had carried since childhood. I would sit across from her, sometimes joining in with my untrained voice, more often just listening. In those moments, the world felt whole again.

Caregiving for Delfina was different than it had been for Rummy. It wasn't the same long, slow unraveling of memory, but the steady wearing down of the body. Both were hard in their own ways. With Delfina, I had the gift of her mind—her wit, her humor, her sharpness—right up to the end. But I also bore the weight of watching her grow tired, each breathe a little more labored, each step a little more careful.

Even so, she was never without grace. She laughed easily, teased me when I burned something on the stove, and thanked me more often than she needed to. On her hardest days, she still managed a smile. That was Delfina—choosing joy, choosing love, even when life gave her reason to despair.

Her final months were marked by quiet strength. She no longer had the energy for long visits, but she treasured the presence of family. She would sit, listening to conversations swirling around her, her eyes shining though her voice grew faint. I often caught her watching me with that same patient smile, as if she were telling me without words: It's alright. I'm ready. You've done enough.

When the time came, she left as gracefully as she had lived. I was by her side, holding her hand, the steady hiss of her oxygen machine marking the rhythm of her last hours. There was no struggle, only a slow and gentle fading. I whispered prayers, told her how much she was loved, and thanked her for every day we had shared.

Delfina passed in peace, leaving behind a legacy not of grand gestures, but of quiet constancy—songs sung in church, meals shared at the table, laughter that filled the house, and love that carried us all through the hardest years.

I lost her, but I never lost what she gave me. The music of her voice, the warmth of her presence, the way she steadied me, when I was ready to fall—all of it remains. If Rummy taught me about the long goodbye, Delfina taught me about the quiet strength of staying until the very end.

And even now, I still hear her voice in the hymns at church, still picture her hands on the piano keys, still feel her presence in the silence of our home. She is gone, but she is everywhere.

After Delfina's passing, the house felt different—quieter, heavier, as though the music had been turned down and the laughter had stepped into another room. Yet, I was not left with emptiness. I was left with memories, with lessons, with love poured into me by two remarkable women. Their absence was painful, but their presence was still everywhere—woven into the walls of our home, the faces of our family, the very rhythm of my days. And so, even in loss, life continued. My story was not finished, and neither was theirs, for they lived on in me.

Chapter 20
Reflections after the Long Goodbye

The house was never the same after both Rummy and Delfina were gone. The silence felt heavier, as if the music and laughter that once filled the rooms had stepped quietly into another place. Yet even in that silence, I was not alone. Their presence lingered in a thousand ways—the photographs on the walls, the worn keys of Delfina's piano, the faint trace of Rummy's perfume in a drawer. They were gone, but they were everywhere.

Looking back, I see how much of my life became defined by caregiving. Years of rising in the middle of the night, living in fragments of sleep, always alert. My body bore the exhaustion, but my heart carried something greater—the privilege of being there, of seeing them through to the end with dignity and love. Caregiving is a hard road, but it is also sacred ground. It teaches you what love really means: not the easy days, but the ones when love endures without return.

Rummy taught me patience I never knew I had. She showed me that love doesn't vanish when memory fades. Even when she looked at me and didn't know my name, I still knew hers, and I carried it for both of us. Through her, I learned to treasure small moments—the feel of her hand in mine, the rare spark of recognition, the tenderness she showed April, her rag doll. She taught me what it means to keep a vow: for better or worse, in sickness and in health, until the very end.

Delfina taught me the gift of presence. Her body grew weak, but her spirit remained sharp, steady, and grateful. She laughed with me, scolded me when I pushed too hard, and filled our home with music even when her breath was short. She showed me that strength isn't always loud—it can be quiet, graceful, and full of joy. Her gratitude on the hardest days reminded me never to take a moment for granted.

When both sisters were gone, I had to adjust not only to their absence but also to the sudden stillness in my own life. After years of being needed every moment, I woke to days that were mine again. It was strange at first. I caught myself listening for footsteps or waiting to hear Delfina humming in the other room. But I came to understand that the silence wasn't empty—it was full of memory. Every corner of the house still carried their voices, their laughter, their love.

Family helped fill the space. Children, grandchildren, and great-grandchildren kept me connected to the living legacy Rummy and Delfina left behind. Watching them grow, I see pieces of both women reflected in the next generations—Rummy's fire, Delfina's grace, their shared strength of spirit. The love that began with them did not end with them. It carries forward in all of us.

And so, even after the long goodbye, my story was not finished. Theirs wasn't either. They live on in the way I carry myself, in the way I love others, in the way I tell this story. Writing these pages is not just remembering—it is giving them back to the world, so their lives are not forgotten.

If Rummy showed me the long goodbye, and Delfina showed me the quiet strength of staying, then together they taught me this: love endures longer than loss. I will always miss them, but I will never stop carrying them. Their story is my story—and through me, it continues.

Chapter 21
Wings of Memory

After Delfina passed, I didn't know who I was anymore.

Not in the way that you question your name or where you come from—but in the quiet, aching spaces where your purpose used to live.

For years, I had been a caregiver. First for Rummy, then for Delfina. Their needs shaped my days. Their love shaped my life.

And when that was gone… the silence was too loud. The stillness too sharp.

But grief doesn't just take—it waits.

It waits for the day you find enough strength to breathe differently. To do one small thing that reminds you that you're still here. Still living. Still allowed to feel joy.

For me, that moment came about a year after Delfina was gone.

I picked up my drone controller.

I had set it aside during those caregiver years. There just wasn't time—or heart—for hobbies. But something told me that day: go fly.

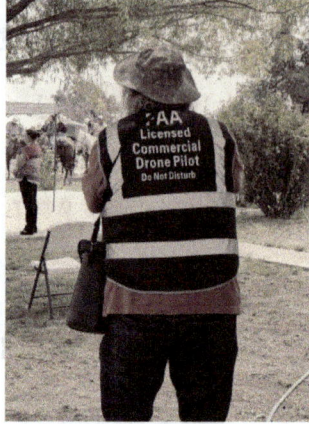

A few of my Drones

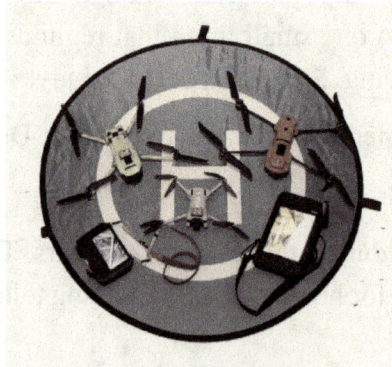

Me as a Drone Pilot

I took it out to the edge of town. Let the blades spin. Watched it lift into the air.

And there it was—the view from above.

The sky. The horizon. The rooftops of our quiet little town.

From up there, everything seemed calmer. Smaller. Sacred.

I imagined her watching from just beyond the clouds. I imagined what she might say:

"Don't you dare crash that thing."

Or maybe: "Are you serious, Ralph?"

That made me smile.

***

I started putting her favorite songs to my flight videos. Songs like *"There Could Never Be Another Love for Me but You"* by John Berry. That one hit hard.

The melody, the lyrics—they were us.

Sometimes, I'd match the drone's graceful movements to the rise and fall of the music. Other times, I just let the wind take it.

And the people who watched… they felt it.

They saw her spirit in the clouds, in the light, in the way the drone hovered gently above places she once walked.

One day, I made a memorial video just of her photos.

I set it to "Dancing in the Sky."

I cried the entire time I edited it.

But they were good tears. Healing tears.

***

It's strange how flight, something so mechanical, brought me closer to something divine.

The sky became my chapel. The drone, my prayer.

Each flight is a conversation.

Each song, a love letter.

I'll never stop missing her. Or Rummy.

123

There won't be another love like that for me in this lifetime.

But I carry them both in every sunrise, in every kitchen recipe, every quiet Sunday, every song, and every flight.

***

They say grief never really goes away.

But I think that's because love doesn't, either.

And if love is still here... so are they.

Epilogue: For Those Who Loved, Lost, and Loved Again

If you've made it this far, thank you.

Thank you for walking beside me through the joy, the heartbreak, the laughter, and the long goodbyes.

This wasn't just a story about being married to two sisters.

It was a story about love—real love—the kind that doesn't quit when things get hard, or when memory fades, or when illness takes away everything except the heart.

It was about devotion, and the quiet heroism of care. About becoming a husband, a stepfather, a caregiver, a cook, a nurse, a handyman, and—eventually—a widower.

It was about grief, yes. But more than that, it was about how grief is born from deep love. You don't grieve what didn't matter. You don't cry for something that wasn't beautiful.

So, if you're grieving… know that means you loved well.

And if you're loving someone through illness… know that every meal you make, every hand you hold, every tired breath you witness—it matters more than words can ever express.

I was honored to be Rummy's husband for 36 years. I was blessed to love Delfina until her last breath. And I'm grateful to have been loved so fully by both.

If there's anything I hope you take from this story, it's that love isn't limited to one chapter, one person, or one lifetime.

Love stretches.

It deepens.

It survives the unspeakable.

And in the end, it lifts us higher than we ever thought we could go—sometimes, all the way to the sky, with a drone, a song, and a prayer.

I'll keep flying for them.

I'll keep loving in their memory.

And if you're still reading this... maybe, just maybe, you will too.

With gratitude,

Ralph

About the Author

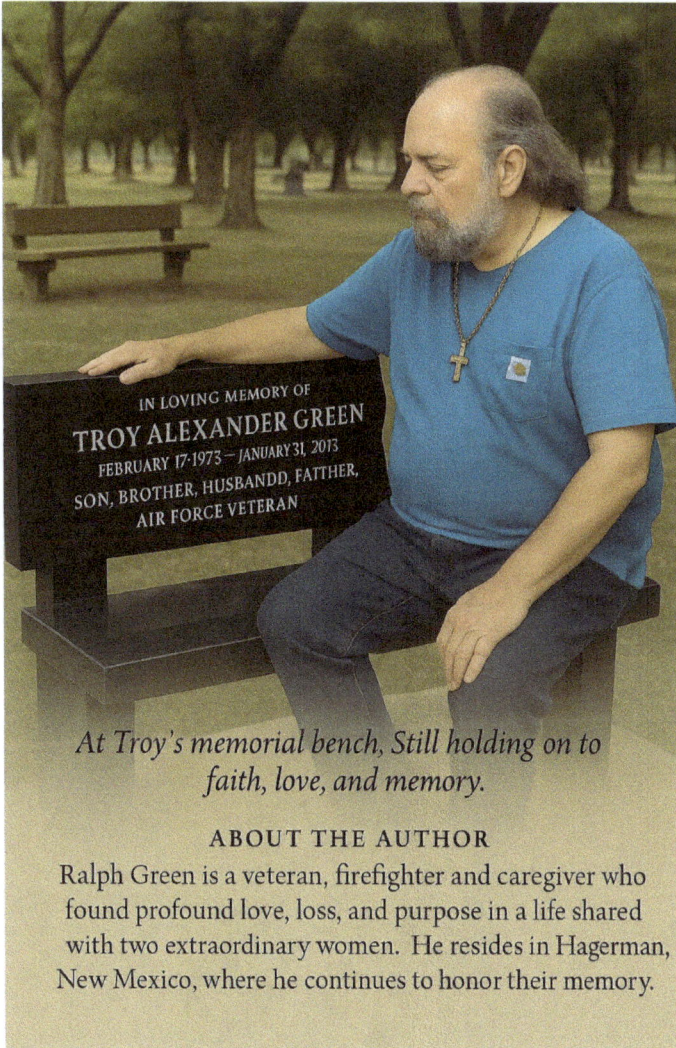

At Troy's memorial bench, Still holding on to faith, love, and memory.

ABOUT THE AUTHOR

Ralph Green is a veteran, firefighter and caregiver who found profound love, loss, and purpose in a life shared with two extraordinary women. He resides in Hagerman, New Mexico, where he continues to honor their memory.

Appendix

These are links to personal videos that are relevant to my story that I would like to share with my readers.

First, "Libro Abierto." The last song Delfina and I got to sing together. Shortly after we did this video, she became too weak to sing, or hold her guitar.

Scan the QR to view the Video for Libro Abierto

Scan the QR code to view Larry's video

Scan the QR code to view Troy's video

www.ingramcontent.com/pod-product-compliance
Lightning Source LLC
LaVergne TN
LVHW021122080426
835513LV00011B/1196